FOOTBALL ACCORDING TO
KLOPP

HIS TACTICAL EVOLUTION AND TRAINING ACTIVITIES

ALEJANDRO GÓMEZ ESCOLAR

FOOTBALL ACCORDING TO KLOPP / Alejandro Gómez Escolar- 1st edition
LIBROFUTBOL.com, 2022.

184 pages; 15,2 x 22,9 cm.

ISBN 978-987-8943-47-3

1. Football.
CDD 796.334077

FOOTBALL ACCORDING TO KLOPP
by Alejandro Gómez Escolar

Cover: Luciano Medvetkin Analysis tools: © InStat	Photo of the author: © Alejandro Gómez Escolar Cover photo: © Gonzales Photo / Alamy Stock Photo
© 2022 –Alejandro Gómez Escolar © 2022 – LIBROFUTBOL.com	**All rights reserved**
The partial or total reproduction, storage, rental, transmission or transformation of this book, in any form or by any means, electronic or mechanical, by photocopying, digitization or other methods, is not allowed without prior written permission from the publisher. Any violation is punishable by law.	
ISBN 978-987-8943-47-3	1st edition: September 2022

ediciones@librofutbol.com

+54 9 11 2215 1982

librofutbol

Av. Libertador 6898 - Núñez - City of Buenos Aires - Argentina

Index

Introduction

Jürgen Klopp (born June 16, 1967) is not just another football coach. He shines with a light of his own. For this reason, when one begins to analyze this German coach, one must begin by understanding that emotion and reason are complementary elements. Klopp cannot be understood as a tactician without also understanding Klopp as a person. The success of his philosophy can be explained according to three pillars: his personality, his creation of a cultural identity, and his tactical doctrine.

Klopp is not interested in conventions or consensus. Behind that luminous and genuine smile is a sincere person with clear ideas and unbridled passions. He has an intrinsic communicative drive. He speaks from the heart and with the conviction that characterizes other great persuaders. His words are always accompanied by expressive gestures which, along with his charisma and authenticity, makes him an easy person to connect with. His ability to make himself easily understood by all has earned him many fans and made him one of the most followed and admired icons in world football.

Klopp has his own way of doing things. For him, "life is a matter of relationships" (2019) and therefore managing the human factor is essential. His coaching career has earned him a reputation as a rejuvenator of clubs. When he took charge at Borussia Dortmund and Liverpool, both clubs were in decline. The German coach has been able to revive them and has reshaped them into powerhouses of their time. To a large extent, this capacity for rebuilding is due to the creation and management of a cultural identity. As Pepijn Lijnders, one of his main assistants at Liverpool, recognized in 2017; "Klopp creates a family." The success of his method lies in the fact that "30% is tactics and 70% is team building."

In this way, he encourages all the people who work with and for the club to feel a part of the group from day one, especially the players themselves. Klopp believes that this is the ideal context for the players to feel understood, supported, and free to give their best. In this way he is able to inspire an essential sense of belonging so that the squad, the club, and the fans all push in the same direction.

These personality traits are reflected in the way he understands football. Speed, energy, and high intensity inundate the core aspects of his game model. When in possession of the ball, Klopp's teams are characterized by their ability to progress quickly and vertically, applying the concepts of width and depth, dominating the opponent's half of the field, and generating abundant scoring chances, whether by breaking down the opponent's back line or through counterattacks.

However, in a departure from the offensive Image commonly associated with his style, Klopp believes that the team must be built on defense first. For the German coach, training the defensive phase is a priority, since "it does not depend as much on the talent of the players as it does on their character and willingness to learn and work hard" (quoted by Neveling, 2016). Jürgen's teams aim to attack by winning the ball back as soon as possible. Although they have mastered defending in all three blocks (high, medium and low), his teams' greatest hallmarks are pressing with high intensity after losing possession and counterattacking, two points that are integrated into the concept of *gegenpressing*.

The successful application of the Klopp method has several requirements. It's a style that demands great physical and mental strength. The Stuttgart-born coach has a preference for energetic players who are capable of physical exertion both in normal moments of high intensity and for prolonged periods of time during high-tempo matches. Likewise, they must have a "monster mentality" (Klopp, cited by Lijnders, 2022). That is to say: he prioritizes players with character and a collective attitude who can implement and feel his philosophy of the game, and approach each match as if it were a final.

Harmonizing all these elements leads to what Klopp considers the true source of success: having the best plan. This strategy is based on the holistic functioning of the collective. "It's not about having the best players individually, but how good you can be as a team" (Klopp, quoted by Neveling, 2016). In this sense, according to Lijnders, the German coach does not aspire to "be the best team in the world, but to have the ability to beat the best in the world in its own way."

In this book, the reader will find an in-depth analysis of Klopp's playing patterns at Borussia Dortmund and Liverpool. A methodological analysis based on the four moments of the game has been followed: the offensive phase, the defensive transition, the defensive phase, and the offensive transition. Through reasoned explanations supported by Images, one will be able to understand how his teams work.

Football is a game of variables, full of uncertainty. I will seldom attend to dogmas, but rather to interpretations of players and particular contexts. At no time am I attempting to deal in absolutes. Instead, I will expose and propose ideas. The intention of this book is to draw the reader in and make Klopp's work understandable from a purely tactical perspective. I hope you enjoy it.

Analysis of the phases of the game at Borussia Dortmund

Jürgen Klopp's career at Borussia Dortmund spanned from the 2008/09 to 2014/15 seasons. In those seven years, the German coach managed to rebuild the competitive fortunes of the club and re-established it among the elite of European football.

Klopp's time at Borussia Dortmund can be broken down into three stages. During the first two seasons (2008 to 2010) he laid the foundations of the team's identity and his playing philosophy, and filled the squad with players who fit both. In those years some pillars of his future team began to be established, such as fullback Marcel Schmelzer, midfielders Sven Bender and Nuri Sahin, and attackers Kevin Großkreutz and Mario Götze. In the following campaign there was another leap in quality with the additions of fullback Łukasz Piszczek and attackers Shinji Kagawa and Robert Lewandowski. This launched a second boom phase that spanned four consecutive years (from 2010 to 2014). In this period, Klopp managed to create a young and vigorous team capable of overcoming any opponent. They won the Bundesliga twice, including the first double in club history, and reached the Champions League final against Bayern München in 2013. Ultimately, uneven results in the 2014/15 season meant that the team did not meet their goals and Klopp ended his time at the club.

Offensive phase

Systems

Although Klopp used several systems in the offensive phase throughout his seven years at Borussia Dortmund, such as the 1-4-4-2 with a diamond midfield and the 1-4-3-3, his trademark was the 1-4-2-3-1. The German coach was one of the greatest exponents of this system in European football, using it in 79% of his club games (according to transfermarkt.com). He employed it for two main reasons. In the first place, it allowed him to play with four attackers: compared to the 1-4-3-3, it substituted a midfielder for an additional forward. Likewise, it made it possible to have five lines of players distributed at different heights. Secondly, and as a consequence of its characteristics, this structure adapted perfectly to the dynamic demands of Klopp's game model.

As for that 1-4-2-3-1, the actual arrangement of players during the offensive phase in the opponent's half of the field became a 1-3-3-3-1. As can be seen in Image 1, one of the midfielders, in this case Sebastian Kehl (5), drops down to generate superiorities in the first line. The fullbacks Schmelzer (29) and Piszczek (26) move up and occupy maximum width, while the wingers Großkreutz (19) and Jakub Błaszczykowski (16) move inside to create advantages behind the opposing midfielders along with the attacking midfielder Kagawa (23) and the center forward Lewandowski (9), who serve to fix the opposing central defenders.

Image 1. Bundesliga 2011/12: Borussia Dortmund–Bayern München

Organized attack

STARTING ZONE

In the game model of Klopp's Borussia Dortmund, the primary responsibility for bringing the ball out of the back fell to the central defenders, when playing out both short and long. The first line of pressure of most opponents protected the central channel, so the centerbacks would be positioned in the interior channels (channels 2 and 4). Positioned in this way, both had fewer obstacles in front of them and were in a more advantageous position to thread balls within the intervals of the opponent's midfield line. The main idea was to play as few passes as possible in the first third of the field. Due to his game model, Klopp's Borussia Dortmund would arrange between seven and eight players in front of the ball, which meant that a loss of possession by the first line could allow the opponent to progress directly on goal.

The priority for Klopp was to reach the opponent's goal as quickly as possible. Therefore, he demanded that his central defenders looked for vertical passes to the free man behind the opposing midfielders as the first option. This can be seen in Image 2, in an action where the left centerback Mats Hummels (15) makes a vertical pass in the same interior channel to the left winger Großkreutz (19), who is positioned between the lines to take advantage of the free space generated when the opposing midfielder steps up to pressure.

Image 2. Champions League final 2012/13: Borussia Dortmund–Bayern München

However, when facing zonal defending in a medium block that didn't press, it was common for either of the two central defenders to drive with the ball through an interior channel until they attracted an opponent, at which point they would pass to the free man appearing behind him. This can be seen in Image 3: the left centerback Sokratis Papastathopoulos (25) advances to fix the opposing midfielder Julian Baumgartlinger (14) and then plays a pass behind him to the right winger Kevin Kampl (23).

Image 3. Bundesliga 2014/15: Borussia Dortmund–Mainz 05

In the game model of Klopp's Borussia Dortmund, the fullbacks fulfilled functions of the utmost importance. They were responsible for providing width, occupying the outer channels (1 and 5) by themselves, and attacking the back line from the outside. During the initial years they adopted different heights depending on the positioning of the opposing defenders. Against medium blocks defending in their own half of the field, as can be seen in Image 4 with the left back Schmelzer (29), they would drop back sufficiently to separate from their marker, who in this example is the right winger Patrick Herrmann (15), and provide an outside passing option for the centerback.

Image 4. Bundesliga 2010/11: Borussia Dortmund–Borussia Mönchengladbach

Once the ball reached the outer channels, the fullback would decide whether to play an outside-out pass (in the same channel) to the winger out wide or, as was more typical, progress with an outside-in pass (from the outside channel to an inside channel).

This type of connection could have two intentions. On one hand, to continue progression on the outside and generate a 2-vs-1 superiority against the rival winger. This can be seen in Image 5, in which the right fullback Piszczek (26) executes a wall pass with the player in the interior channel, who in this case is the right midfielder İlkay Gündoğan (8), occupying the space behind the opposing striker on the strong side. If this midfielder receives the pass with a good body position, he can progress with the ball himself, without having to return the wall pass to the player in the outside channel.

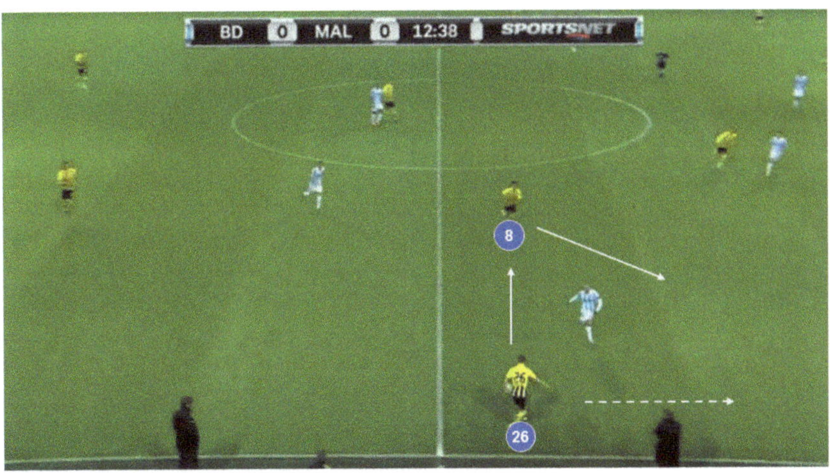

Image 5. Champions League quarter-final 2012/13: Borussia Dortmund–Málaga

On the other hand, as seen in Image 6, they could also thread passes into an inside channel behind the opponent's midfield line. In this similar situation, the right back Piszczek (26) finds the right midfielder Bender (22) as he dismarks into space in the interior channel.

Image 6. Champions League group stage 2011/12: Arsenal–Borussia Dortmund

During his early seasons with the team, Klopp used to propose a short buildout through the fullbacks. However, he gradually realized that these players were more useful if he kept them up high in the opponent's half of the field, between the opponent's defensive and midfield lines. Finding the fullbacks in this context made it possible to continue progression through the outer channels after overcomming two opposing lines of pressure with just two passes, while also having an additional attacking player in the opposing half.

Therefore, the player in the interior channel behind the opposing midfielders began to serve as a third man to deliver the ball to the fullbacks. That third man was typically a winger who had moved inside, as we see the right winger Błaszczykowski (16) do in Image 7. However, this task could also fall to the attacking midfielder or the center forward, dropping down to support. Threading a pass inside would cause the defense to narrow and provide additional space that could be exploited on the outside.

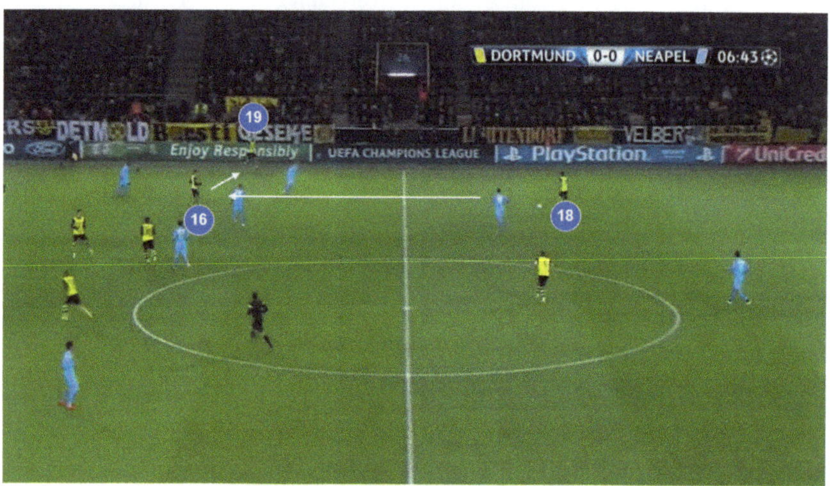

Image 7. Champions League group stage 2013/14: Borussia Dortmund–Napoli

As a consequence, Klopp preferred to generate superiorities with the first line through mechanisms involving the midfielders. Initially, he was looking for situations of 3-vs-2 numerical superiority against opponents with two forwards, placing one of his midfielders in an intermediate position behind both forwards, as shown in Image 8. In this way a central midfielder, in this case Gündoğan (21), would be able to attract the two attackers, which would always leave a free player who could overcome that front row. If the opponent stepped up to the central defender with the ball, Neven Subotić (4) in this sequence, this player could escape that situation by passing the ball, since an adequate distance was maintained between the two centerbacks, as seen with Hummels (15) in Image 8. Therefore, if the forward marking the midfielder steps up, as Thomas Müller (25) does in this case, the center midfielder Gündoğan (21) would made a movement perpendicular to the path of the pressure and create a passing line with the centerback being pressed.

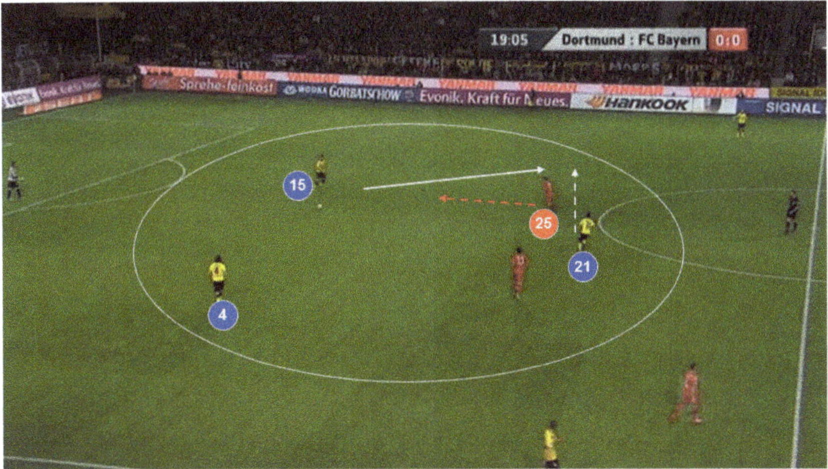

Image 8. Bundesliga 2011/12: Borussia Dortmund–Bayern München

Given that this supporting movement was generally made to the sides of the rival forwards, taking advantage of the space created by the height of the fullbacks, the midfielder responsible for creating superiority would take up a wide position where he could receive the ball while facing forward. More often than not, the midfielder with the best passing technique would be the one to offer this support. In this way, they always managed to have superiority in the first line: 3-vs-1 against rivals with one forward, as seen in Image 9, and 3-vs-2 when playing against two forwards.

Image 9. Champions League semi-final 2012/13: Borussia Dortmund–Real Madrid

The position of the other midfielder also played an important role, depending on the opponent's pressing behavior. Both central midfielders would look to be positioned at different heights. Against opponents who marked the defensive midfielder in the buildout, as can be seen with Gündoğan (21) in Image 10, he would offer himself as a threat behind and between the opponents on the forward line. In this way he would draw his marker in to create a 4-vs-3 situation in his own half of the field. This scenario was typically resolved by running with the ball through the interior channels or by threading a pass into the free space generated when the opposing midfielder stepped up.

Image 10. Bundesliga 2011/12: Borussia Dortmund–Bayern München

In scenarios where the opponent played with a passive zonal defense (that is: without stepping up on players in possession who were outside the defensive structure), a midfielder would be located in that same position, providing an option to progress short by overcoming the first defensive line, or would look to get behind the second line, as Gündoğan (21) does in Image 11.

Image 11. Bundesliga 2011/12: Borussia Dortmund–Bayern München

Depopulating the center of his offensive structure was never a concern for Klopp. In fact, since his intention was to play passes to the more advanced players and skip the midfield line, this mechanism fit perfectly with his game model and became his most frequently used buildout scheme.

Although playing out short from the first third of the field was the priority, especially in the Bundesliga where his team had higher percentages of possession (an average of 52.5% in Klopp's seven years, according to whoscored.com) than it did in European competitions, he often alternated this pattern with long direct play. This option was used if no progress could be made after a sequence of side-to-side passes, when under pressure from a high block (whether it was frontal pressing or the ball was steered towards the outer channels), or if an advantageous situation materialized along the opponent's back line.

During Klopp's first three years, the starting center forwards were Nelson Haedo Valdez (2008 to 2009) and Lucas Barrios (2008 to 2010). Later, that spot in the linup was taken over by Lewandowski (2011 to 2014). These were all players with great physical power and dexterity when playing with their backs to goal, who offered multiple variants when playing long. When the centerbacks decided to play direct, they always looked to attack the back line. Whoever played the center forward role would almost always occupy the central channel, although he could also sporadically fall back into the inside channels. If he managed to receive cleanly, he would be able to protect the ball and hold it in a static position or play as the third man to lay it off to an attacking midfielder or winger coming inside.

In the event that the long delivery resulted in an aerial duel against the back line, one of the offensive teammates would attack the free space being generated in search of a flick-on. In the first three seasons, a midfielder would undertake this function. After that, the wingers took over this role, as can be seen in Image 12. In that sequence, this behavior is reflected in the diagonal movement of the left winger Großkreutz (19) towards the central channel just before the center forward Lewandowski (7) challenges for the ball.

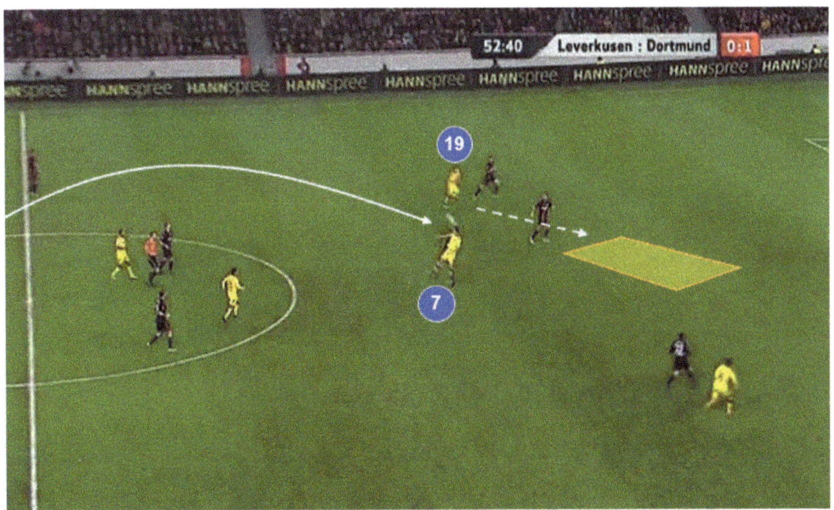

Image 12. Bundesliga 2010/11: Bayer Leverkusen–Borussia Dortmund

Their direct play was not just about the moment of the aerial duel, but also about the second ball in the active zone. In this facet of the game, Klopp worked very hard at Borussia Dortmund so that the nearby players would position themselves for that challenge, in front of their opponents to win the ball after it dropped. They did not always need to win the aerial battle: good positioning for the subsequent action allowed them to generate quick attacks in the opponent's half of the field that were difficult to defend.

However, not all long balls in the buildout were intended to generate an aerial duel. Sometimes these deliveries were aimed at a space and not at a player. As can be seen in Image 13, in his first seasons at Borussia Dortmund Klopp used systems with two strikers and frequently one of these forwards, in this case Mohamed Zidan (10), would drop down to support in the same channel as the ball. If he managed to drag his marker with him, the other center forward, here Valdez (9), would attack the gap that was generated.

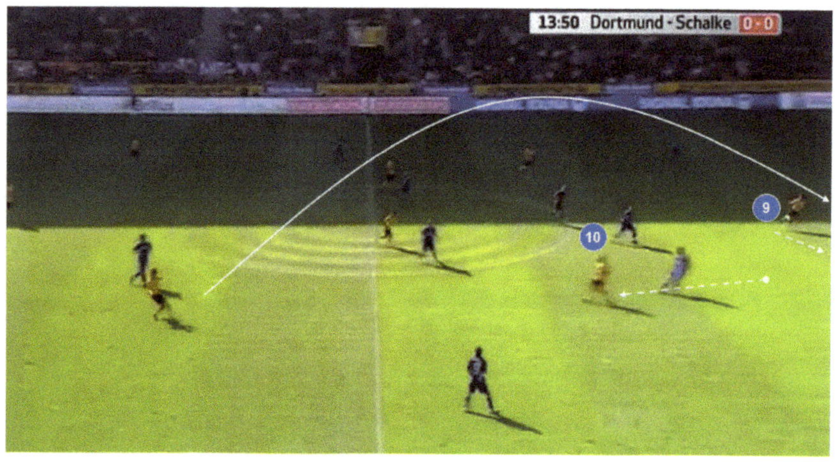

Image 13. Bundesliga 2008/09: Borussia Dortmund–Schalke 04

Against defenses who pushed their back line up high, Klopp's squad could also play directly to the zone of offensive advantage. As can be seen in Image 14, the attackers would position themselves at the same height as the opponent's back line and within the intervals, with the aim of making runs in behind them in situations of 3-vs-4 numerical inferiority. This type of Situation, where the more distant players would offer the player in possession an option to pass into space, were often also triggered by the weak side fullback during a switch of play.

Image 14. Bundesliga 2013/14: Borussia Dortmund–Hamburg

During the 2014/15 season, after Lewandowski's departure to Bayern München, Pierre-Emerick Aubameyang became the starting center forward. Although the Gabonese could engage in aerial duels, this was not his main physical virtue. For this reason, long passes went mostly into space. As can be seen in Image 15, it was common for Aubameyang (17) to break free from his markers in the interval between a centerback and a fullback. In this way, Klopp tried to take advantage of his speed more efficiently.

Image 15. Bundesliga 2014/15: Borussia Dortmund–Mainz 05

CREATION ZONE

Except for long shots, which would be generated from the middle third of the field, the rest of the mechanisms explained in the starting zone could also be used to attack the space between the opponent's midfield and defensive lines. That space became Klopp's great obsession, as well as the key to his game model in the offensive phase. Playing the ball there meant eliminating six opponents and having only a single line of defenders blocking the path to goal. The team would be able to generate scoring chances with sequences of between two and four passes.

To do this, the team's distribution in the opponent's half of the field consisted of placing six or seven players in front of the ball, looking to generate superiority behind the opposing midfielders. As can be seen in Image 16, the fullbacks, in this case Schmelzer (29) and Piszczek (26), spread out to provide width in the outside channels. The wingers Großkreutz (19) and Błaszczykowski (16) would move into the interior spaces behind the opposing midfielders. This caused constant uncertainty for the opponent's outside defenders, as they faced a double threat: if they chased the wingers, this left free space for the fullbacks to attack out wide; if they held their positions instead, this would allow a pass to be made to the penultimate attacker.

Most of the time the center forward, here Lewandowski (9), would be responsible for fixing the two centerbacks to prevent them from supporting the fullbacks, although he had some freedom to dismark in support by dropping down in the inside channels. In the same way, the attacking midfielder Kagawa (23) would often find himself on the same side as the ball, finding himself unmarked and offering the player in possession a passing line between the defenders' intervals.

Image 16. Bundesliga 2011/12: Borussia Dortmund–Bayern München

The ideal situation would be to have a free player receiving between the lines who could immediately turn and attack the back line. As can be seen in Image 17, a winger, in this case Reus (11) on the left, would be able to take an oriented touch with their far foot and turn with space and time to face the back line. Once the ball would reach that zone, the back-pass ceased to be an option.

Image 17. German Super Cup 2013/14: Borussia Dortmund–Bayern München

If the receiver couldn't turn, he would lay the ball off to a forward-facing third man who would look for another vertical pass to a fourth player. An example of this situation can be seen in Image 18, in which the midfielder Reus (11), after receiving a pass from the central defender, acts as the third man and leaves the ball for the center forward Lewandowski (9), who had dropped down in the outside channel. The Polish attacker quickly plays a long pass to the fourth man; the right back Piszczek (26) advancing on the weak side.

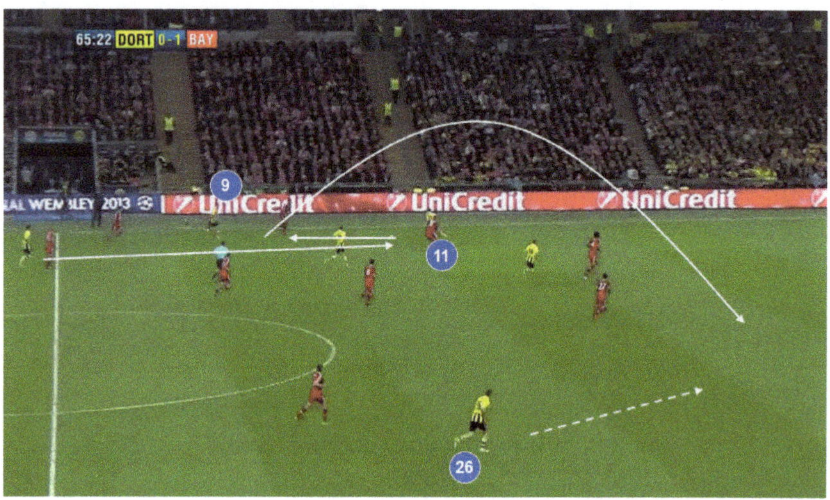

Image 18. Champions League final 2012/13: Borussia Dortmund–Bayern München

But within this area between the lines, the players were allowed freedom of movement and could exchange positions when desired. In this way, Klopp produced a context that fostered the creative and spontaneous expression of his players. In each offensive wave there were constant entry and exit movements and correlated supports and dismarks, which made it difficult for the opponents to defend in a medium block. To maintain a rational distribution of space, Klopp established certain offensive principles in the creation zone.

If an opponent from the midfield line stepped up to the player in possession, a player had to occupy that free space, as can be seen in Image 19 with the movement made by the right midfielder Miloš Jojić (14). That area could also be occupied by the center forward checking back.

Image 19. Champions League quarter-final 2013/14: Borussia Dortmund–Real Madrid

If the fullback occupied the outside channel, the winger had to occupy an inside space, and vice versa. There was always to be at least one player providing width. As can be seen in Image 20, if the right back, here Großkreutz (19), occupies the interior channel then the right winger Błaszczykowski (16) would provide width.

Image 20. German Super Cup 2013/14: Borussia Dortmund–Bayern München

If the winger started from the outside channel and made a movement to the inside, he would look to drag the opponent's outside defender with him to create free space that could be attacked by the fullback. This move was widely used to exploit the weak side with a diagonal switch of play. As Image 21 shows, as soon as the weak side fullback, in this case Piszczek (26) on the right, senses that a long pass was about to be made, he would move up the field, anticipating the play and projecting himself deep into the free space created by the outside-in movement of the right winger, here Błaszczykowski (16), who has dragged his marker with him.

Image 21. Champions League quarter-final 2012/13: Borussia Dortmund—Málaga

If the opponent's outside defender stepped up to the wide player, as happens here with the right back Piszczek (26), one of the inside players, in this case the attacking midfielder Götze (10), would attack the interval between the centerback and the fullback with a run in behind. This movement could be made to receive a through pass, as seen in Image 22.

Image 22. Champions League quarter-final 2012/13: Borussia Dortmund–Málaga

However, this movement could also have the purpose of dragging an opposing midfielder away to create a free space that could be attacked by the player in the central channel, in situations where the opponent has closed the interior passing lines well. This mechanism was common during Klopp's first years at Borussia Dortmund, in which he employed center forwards dropping down to support.

An example of this can be seen in Image 23: with the right fullback Antonio Rukavina (14) in possession of the ball, the right winger Jakub Błaszczykowski (16) carries out an inside-out movement to create a gap that would allow the center forward Valdez (9) to drop down and receive the ball. At that moment, the attacker would decide whether to lay the ball off or play into space for the winger.

Image 23. UEFA Cup 2008/09: Borussia Dortmund–Udinese

The center forward and the attacking midfielder needed to occupy different channels. As we have seen, the most common method was for the center forward to fix the rival centerbacks in the central channel, allowing the attacking midfielder to operate unmarked. However, these two players could also swap positions.

FINISHING ZONE

The tactical arrangement of the players in the opposing half of the field determined the manner of attacking in the final third. As can be seen in Image 24, the interior positioning of the wingers, in this case Großkreutz (19) and Błaszczykowski (16), and of the center forward Lewandowski (9) caused the rival fullbacks to close in to maintain a 4-vs-3 numerical superiority. Otherwise, the opponent would run too great a risk of allowing 3-vs-3 situations on the inside, too close to the penalty area and against players with the abundance of technical and tactical ability needed to attack space.

Image 24. Bundesliga 2011/12: Borussia Dortmund–Bayern München

Therefore it was originally in the outside channels where the spaces and the free players, the fullbacks, could be found. The most common way for Klopp's Borussia Dortmund to deal with these low block defenses was to run with the ball into the outside channels to force their opponents to make a decision. The big handicap was that neither of their usual fullbacks, Piszczek or Schmelzer, had the ability to eliminate their opponent in 1-vs-1 situations. These players were more dangerous when running into space; ie: attacking empty areas. keeping this in mind, whenever they received the ball their first option tended to be a cross into the box, regardless of whether they were alone or faced with a 1-vs-1 situation.

If a winger received the ball in an outside channel, a 2-vs-2 situation would be generated with the fullback. This could be resolved with a wall pass, as seen in Image 25 where the right winger Błaszczykowski (16) combines with the right fullback Piszczek (26). It could also be resolved through an overlap on the outside, as shown in the action of Image 26, with the right back Piszczek (26) overtaking the right winger Błaszczykowski (16).

Image 25. Champions League final 2012/13: Borussia Dortmund–Bayern München

Image 26. Champions League semi-final 2012/13: Borussia Dortmund–Real Madrid

Klopp also has a preference for attacking space. As can be seen in Image 27, by sending the ball to the fullbacks, in this case Piszczek (26) on the right, the team would seek to lure the opponent's outside defenders into stepping up, fixing them to open up the interval between the centerback and the fullback on that side. This would open up a gap that could be attacked by an inside player. Generally the wingers, like Błaszczykowski (16) on the right in this example, were the closest players to that area, as they were occupying the interior channels nearby, and they would frequently carry out inside-out dismarking movements. Klopp exploited this mechanism over and over again. It was one of the strategies that generated the most goals for his Borussia Dortmund team.

Image 27. Champions League semi-final 2012/13: Borussia Dortmund—Real Madrid

As we have previously observed, it was common for progression to take place through the interior channels or through the central channel via vertical passes. In those situations, Klopp's Borussia Dortmund would get behind the defensive line using two mechanisms.

First, through simple runs in behind. Once a player on the ball managed to face the last line of defenders, the rest of the attackers would place themselves in positions at the edge of the offside line in the interval between the center backs, as the left winger Reus (11) does in Image 28.

Image 28. Champions League group stage 2014/15: Borussia Dortmund–Galatasaray

As can be seen in Image 29, the wingers would also make runs behind the fullback on their side, as we see the left winger Reus (11) do in this example.

Image 29. Bundesliga 2013/14: Borussia Dortmund–Hamburg

If the through-ball was good, this action would very likely result in a 1-vs-1 situation with the goalkeeper. In general, when defending a player driving forward with the ball, most defenders instinctively tend to direct their attention to the immediate threat: the ball. As a consequence they will neglect their mark and alter their body orientation, which allows the attacker to start their run early, and with a positional advantage. At Klopp's Borussia Dortmund, his players were specialists in punishing these situations.

The second mechanism consisted of attacking the zone of offensive advantage by means of dismarks into the free spaces that were generated. This option was used more frequently against opponents with central defenders who would chase their marks.

A gap to be attacked could be created by a player in the same zone as the opposing centerbacks, as can be seen in Image 30. The player closest to the player in possession, here the center forward Lewandowski (9), dismarks to drag his defender away. This generates a free space inside where a teammate can dismark between the centerbacks. In this example, the left winger Reus (11) is the protagonist.

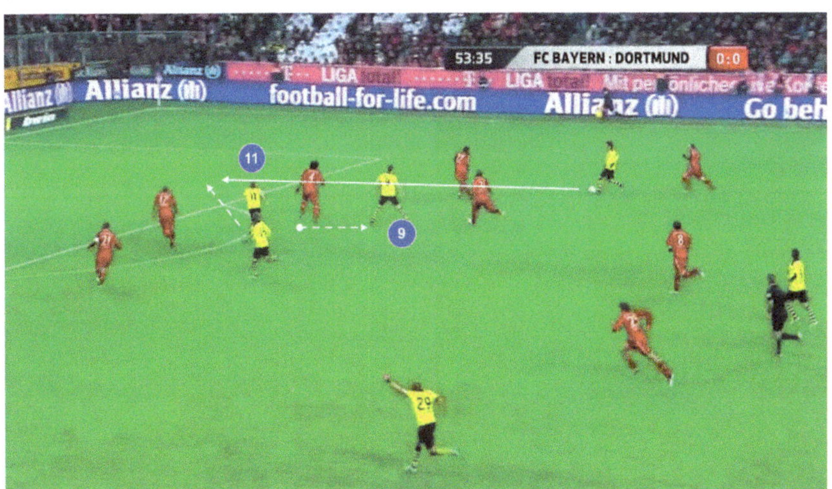

Image 30. Bundesliga 2012/13: Bayern München–Borussia Dortmund

On the other hand, the space generated in the opposing centerbacks' zone could also be exploited by an exterior player.

The action in Image 31 shows how in some situations the center forward, in this case Lewandowski (9), and the left winger Reus (11) would seek to drag defenders from their zone with false supporting dismarks. This would create free space in the central channel for the wide offensive players to attack, either with an outside-in dismark, as the right winger Julian Schieber (23) exectutes in this action, or through a wall pass as the attacking midfielder Götze (10) does.

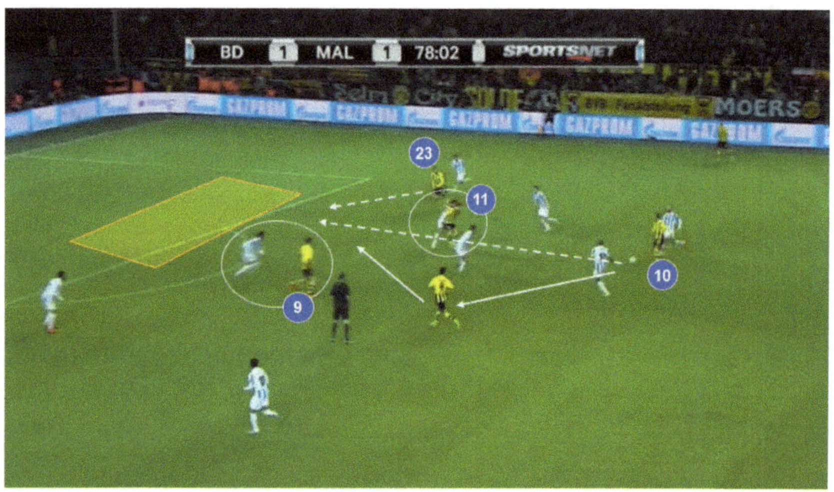

Image 31. Champions League quarter-final 2012/13: Borussia Dortmund–Málaga

As we can see, Klopp's Borussia Dortmund was a team with many options for attacking in the finishing zone. To their aggressive methods of attacking space we must add crosses from the fullbacks. These crosses were not the main formula for getting the ball into the box, but they did provide a significant supply of scoring chances. During their seven years with the Stuttgart-born coach in charge, the team from the west of Germany averaged 18.5 crosses from their fullbacks per game (according to whoscored.com).

In those early seasons Borussia Dortmund used 3 + 1 structures when occupying the penalty area. As can be seen in Image 32, three players would position themselves in the three shooting zones: at the near post is the center forward, who in this case was Lewandowski (9); the attacking midfielder Kagawa (23) appears at the penalty spot, and the far post was left to the winger from the weak side, Błaszczykowski (16) in this action. They would be joined by one of the midfielders, here Kehl (5), who covers the space at the top of the penalty area.

Image 32. Bundesliga 2011/12: Borussia Dortmund–Stuttgart

But beginning with the 2012/13 season, the constant mobility of the attackers meant that they often found themselves out of their normal starting positions. Consequently, they would not occupy the usual three shooting areas, and situations of numerical inferiority with only two shooters would be generated. Sometimes only a single option would be sent into the area. As a general rule, the striker would always be in the area when the ball was crossed from out wide. An example of this can be seen in Image 33, in which the center forward Lewandowski (9) and the weak side winger Błaszczykowski (16) are in a situation of 2-vs-3 inferiority. Given this scenario, they would look to anticipate the cross and get behind their markers. This manifests itself in the movement of Lewandowski (9) to cut behind the far centerback.

Image 33. Champions League semi-final 2012/13: Borussia Dortmund–Real Madrid

Often, the center forward would make one of two movements inside the box to gain a positional advantage over his marker. The first, as Lewandowski (9) executes in Image 34, consisted of starting from the penalty spot and adjusting his trajectory to attack the near post, with the intention of staying ahead of his opponent.

Image 34. Bundesliga 2013/14: Borussia Dortmund–Hamburg

The second movement would be to get behind the back of the far centerback or the last defender. This was a way to attack with a positional advantage beyond the opponent's field of vision. In these situations the crosses from out wide would go to the far post, as reflected in Image 35. Both Lewandowski (9), the center forward in this example, and Aubameyang would use this movement to convert many chances inside the penalty area.

Image 35. Bundesliga 2012/13: Stuttgart–Borussia Dortmund

Offensive Transition

The offensive transition was the phase of the game in which Klopp's Borussia Dortmund really distinguished themselves. As we will explore in depth later, the use of the 1-4-4-2 system and its variants in the defensive phase enabled four players to take part in the counterattack. In this way, multiple channels would be covered: the two wingers, starting at the midfield line, would occupy the interior channels while the attacking midfielder and the center forward would do the same in the central channel. Attacking with four players in the offensive transition frequently allowed for the creation of situations of numerical superiority and numerical equality.

Generally, Klopp's Borussia Dortmund would defend in a medium block, so typically the ball would be won in the first two thirds of the pitch. Regardless of the zone where the ball was recovered, the most important thing for the German coach's team was to counterattack quickly before the opponent's defense could reorganize. This last aspect was essential. The priority was not to play a greater or lesser number of passes or to have more or fewer players intervene, but rather for the counterattack to take place in the most advantageous environment with respect to their opponents. That is to say: with space in front of them and against opponents who would be out of position and forced to defend while moving backwards.

For the transition to be effective, it had to be quick and precise. The success of Klopp's Borussia Dortmund in this stage of the game also lay in the ideal characteristics of his attackers. In addition to being fast and technically outstanding, the players required the ability to understand which spaces to attack and to recognize the right time to do it.

All these counterattacks were governed by the following principle: after winning the ball, the first pass had to be forward. If the ball was won in a low block, the team would look for the furthest player, who could then play back to an attacking midfielder. By staying disconnected from the defensive block in his own half of the field during the defensive phase, the center forward was always that distant player who operated as a target: he generally occupied the central channel, which allowed the attack start in that zone.

But as can be seen in Image 36, the center forward, who in this case is Lewandowski (9), could also drop into the interior channels so that he could lay the ball off to the attacking midfielder in the central channel, Mkhitaryan (10) in this example. Once this final player was in possession of the ball, he would decide whether to continue the progression through the central zone or play the ball into free space on the outside.

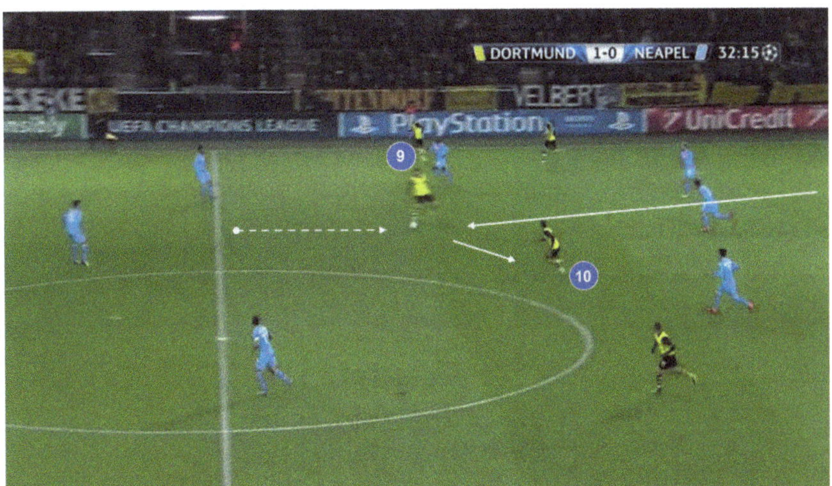

Image 36. Champions League group stage 2013/14: Borussia Dortmund–Napoli

Although it was normal for the center forward to occupy the central channel to act as a target for the first pass, during Klopp's first years this player could also drop down in the outer channels to receive the ball. This movement would be done with the intention of getting away from the centerbacks. In this variant, the first ball would be played long into space. The striker would then hold up the ball so that the rest of the attackers could spread out, or he could look for an individual resolution if he found himself in an advantageous 1-vs-1 or 2-vs-1 situation against the centerbacks. Due to its ineffectiveness, Klopp stopped using this variant.

Once this first phase after recovering the ball was completed, the counterattack would immediately be carried out in the central zone with all three channels being occupied if possible, as can be seen in Image 37. In this way the player running with the ball, the attacking midfielder Reus (11) in this example, has three options and can pass both wide and deep. Likewise, the distances to be covered by the defenders would increase, making it difficult for them to make a decision about who should step up.

Image 37. Champions League final 2012/13: Borussia Dortmund–Bayern München

An option widely used by the attacking midfielders Kagawa, Reus, and Mkhitaryan was to lead the counterattack by running with the ball. This offensive technique allowed them to penetrate directly as the first option. In this situation, the player with the ball would advance down the central channel and the attackers in front of him would make movements to generate space for him. These movements would be diagonal and go from outside to inside. An example is shown in Image 38, in which the right winger Błaszczykowski (16), who finds himself temporarily on the left, makes a move inside that attracts his marker and frees up space for the attacking midfielder Mkhitaryan (10).

Image 38. Champions League group stage 2013/14: Borussia Dortmund–Napoli

Additionally, the player with the ball in these actions could use his run to fix opponents before sending a pass to a free man, generally on the outside. As can be seen in Image 39, a counterattack with a 2-vs-2 numerical equality has developed. The player in possession, here the left winger Reus (11), has the opportunity to carry the ball down the central channel, fixing his defender and laying the ball off for the center forward Lewandowski (9), who finds himself with a 1-vs-1 against the goalkeeper.

Image 39. Champions League quarter-final 2013/14: Borussia Dortmund–Real Madrid

Another of the characteristic movements made by the forwards at Klopp's Borussia was to position themselves behind the last defender in order to stay out of their field of vision. As Aubameyang (17) demonstrates in Image 40, this action allows the center forward to generate a passing line with the player in possession as he also separates from his marker. In this way he can eliminate his opponent with an oriented touch and find himself in a 1-vs-1 situation against the goalkeeper.

Image 40. Bundesliga 2014/15: Borussia Dortmund—Mainz 05

When a player from the second line won the ball in a medium block, the team would progress directly towards the goal with a pass into space, as seen in Image 41. In this example it's the midfielder Kehl (5) who steps up to win the ball, with the center forward Lewandowski (9) exploiting his positional advantage over the two opposing centerbacks to convert the scoring chance.

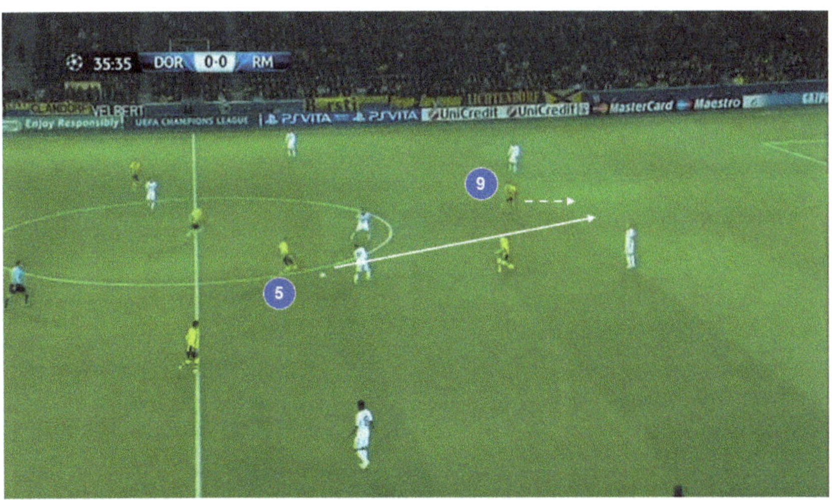

Image 41. Champions League group stage 2012/13: Borussia Dortmund–Real Madrid

To finish their counterattacks, the German coach's players would follow three rules, based on switching channels. If the ball was recovered on the inside, they would finish the play on the outside. To offer context, the opponents typcially prioritized defending the central zones, so there would always be space on the outside. The action in Image 42 starts with the ball being won in a high block in the central zone, in a situation of 5-vs-4 numerical superiority. The left winger Reus (11) runs with the ball until he can fix the last defender and lay the ball off for the center forward Lewandowski (9) to finish from the outside.

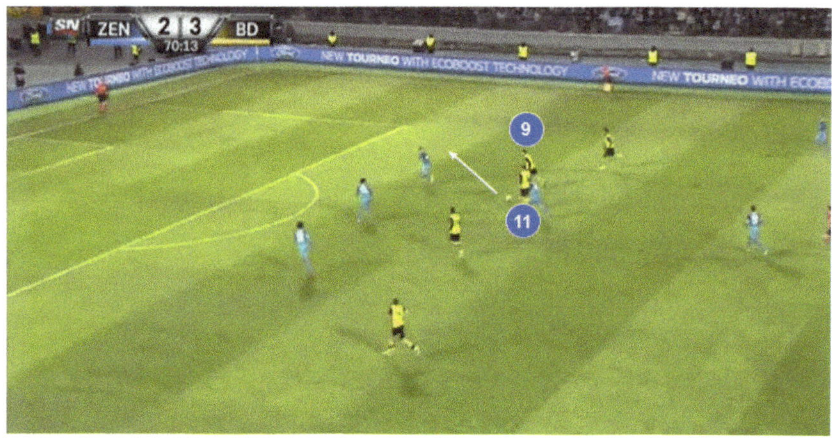

Image 42. Champions League quarter-final 2013/14: Zenit–
Borussia Dortmund

After recovering the ball on the outside, Borussia Dortmund would finish the play on the opposite side. This behavior is shown in Image 43, which begins with them winning the ball in a low block on the left side of the field. The left winger Reus (11) runs with the ball and then passes to the right winger Błaszczykowski (16), who finishes from the opposite wing.

The strategy of ending the attack on the weak side is based on the fact that there is always a lower density of players there.

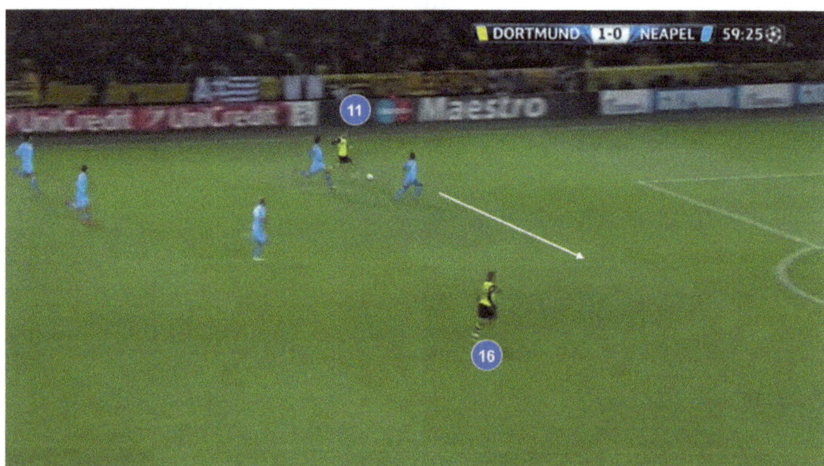

Image 43. Champions League group stage 2013/14: Borussia
Dortmund–Napoli

When the ball was recovered on the outside, the play could also be finished on the inside. Image 44 shows an action that begins with the ball being won in a low block on the left side and ending up at the feet of the left winger Reus (11), who carries the ball forward until he can thread a pass inside for the attacking midfielder Mkhitaryan (10), who finishes from the central channel.

Image 44. Champions League quarter-final 2013/14: Borussia Dortmund—Real Madrid

Defensive phase

Systems

During his time at Borussia Dortmund, Klopp usually defended in a medium block. His most commonly used system was the 1-4-4-2, a formation suitable for defending in the middle third of the field, while playing zonally without pressing the opposing centerbacks. Additionally, the two lines of four allowed the team to shift defensively in order to rationally occupy the field in width and depth. Klopp also preferred to organize his players to support each other defensively and step up from their zones to generate superiorities when the ball was in the wide channels.

Klopp's decision to defend with the 1-4-4-2 system also helped the team to morph into a 1-4-2-3-1 in the offensive transition. In this way, it was only necessary to adjust the position of the wingers, who were required to drop down to reinforce the midfield line in the defensive phase and then surge forward during the counterattack. Depending on the opponent, the German coach would also use other variants such as the 1-4-4-1-1, in order to mark the opponent's central midfielder, or the 1-4-1-4-1 which was used against opponents with mobile players operating between the lines.

Although Klopp rarely imposed high pressure during his first five seasons in Dortmund (from 2008 to 2013), the team maintained its 1-4-4-2 formation when they did. Only in the last two seasons (from 2013 to 2015) did he begin to experiment with high pressing, an aspect of the game that would later optimize his time at Liverpool. He experimented with a 1-4-1-3-2 system against opponents with three central defenders and a 1-4-3-3 formation with players occupying intermediate zones. The common denominator in both cases was the numerical inferiority of the first line of pressure with respect to the opposing defense. Using this as a base, the Stuttgart-born coach began to develop a devotion for defending with players in intermediate zones.

As for defending in a low block, Klopp kept with the 1-4-4-1-1 system throughout his time at Borussia Dortmund. This left the team with two lines of four players operating close together to protect the penalty area, with the center forward disconnected from the defensive block to serve as a target for the counterattack.

Organized defense

HIGH BLOCK

Defensive pressing in a high block was not very common during Klopp's time at Borussia Dortmund. When the team did press high, as a general rule he would use the same system as in the medium block: the 1-4-4-2. When the opposing goalkeeper had the ball, the two attackers (the center forward and the attacking midfielder) maintained a horizontal position, each one keeping track of an opposing defender. As can be seen in Image 45, once the ball reached one of these center backs the nearby player, in this case the attacking midfielder Kagawa (23), would step up on the player in possession while the player farther away, the center forward Lewandowski (9) in this example, would drop down to keep an eye on the opposing midfielder and the far defender from an intermediate position between the two.

This V-shaped rotation would swing if there was a switch of play, with the aim of conserving both their physical efforts and the distances to be covered. If the opponent tried to play a pass inside, a midfielder would step up to the receiver to prevent him from turning and force the ball to be passed backwards, as Kehl (5) does in this sequence. If the ball overcomes his line, the nearby attacker, who in this case is Kagawa (23), closes off the passing line to the nearby centerback and force the opponent to play wide. The winger on the strong side, here Götze (11) on the right, occupies the inside channel and is ready to move outside if the ball is played there. If the opponent's winger shows for an outside-out pass, the fullback on that side would follow to prevent their progression.

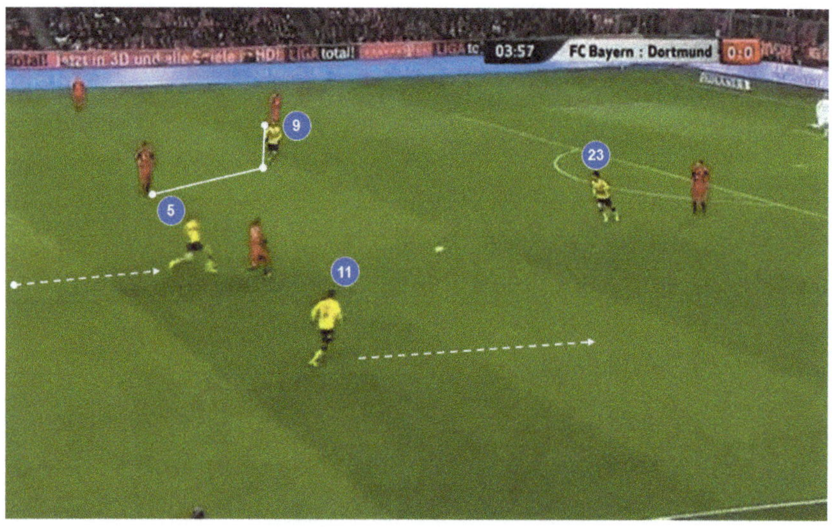

Image 45. Bundesliga 2011/12: Bayern München–Borussia Dortmund

In this way, there would be a situation on the strong side of the ball with all the opponents being marked man-to-man while the weak side would be left open. At that moment, the opponent would have to decide whether to either risk passing inside, play long, or go back to the goalkeeper. In the event that the opponent went back to the goalkeeper, Borussia Dortmund would only put pressure on that player if the centerback made the pass from inside the penalty area. The nearest player applying pressure, in this case Kagawa (23), would exploit his momentum from pressing the defender to continue towards the goalkeeper, taking advantage of the short distance between the two and closing the passing line that could connect the goalkeeper with whoever had passed him the ball. Meanwhile the farther forward, here Lewandowski (9), stops marking the midfielder and begins harassing the other central defender. In addition, the winger on the weak side steps up to the opposing center midfielder, which forces the goalkeeper to play long.

Starting in the 2013/14 season, Klopp began experimenting with a 1-4-1-3-2 system against opponents playing with three defenders. As can be seen in Image 46, the players from the first line —the attacking midfielder, who in this action was Mkhitaryan (10), and the center forward Lewandowski (9)— wait in the intervals between the central defenders for the goalkeeper to decide which side to start on. The wingers, here Reus (11) and Aubameyang (17), would ocupy the interior channels in intermediate positions between the wingbacks and the central midfielders. One of the defensive midfielders, in this case Bender (6), positions himself between the two opposing midfielders. The other, Sahin (18), holds his position to maintain superiority in the defensive line in case the opponent plays long.

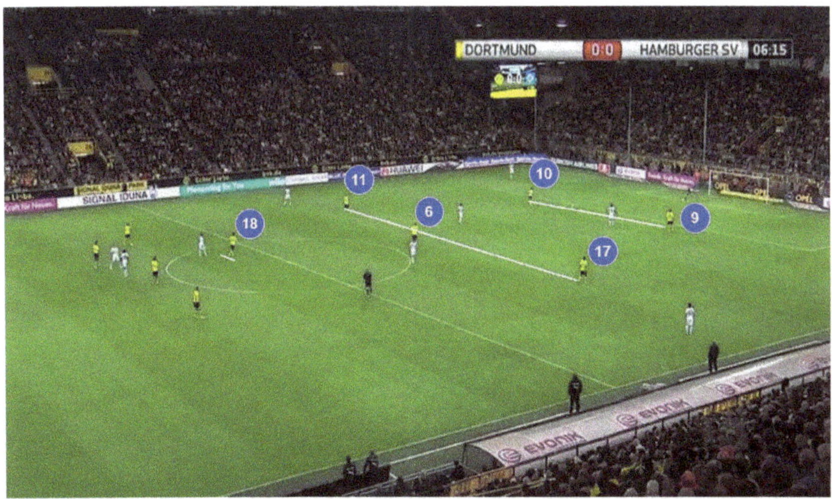

Image 46. Bundesliga 2013/14: Borussia Dortmund–Hamburg

As soon as the goalkeeper plays to a centerback, the matchups begin with the player on the strong side. The closest attacker, who in this action is Mkhitaryan (10), steps up on the player with a bent run, directing the play to the outside and preventing the ball from being passed back to the goalkeeper. The other attacker Lewandowski (9) marks the middle centerback. The winger on the strong side, here Reus (11), steps up on the wingback while the most advanced midfielder Bender (6) matches up with the defensive midfielder. Aubameyang (17), the winger on the weak side, closes in to mark the opposing center midfielder.

The wingback and the centerback on the weak side would be left free. As with the 1-4-4-2 system, Klopp was looking to steer the buildout to one side, match up numerically with the opponent, and leave the opposite side open. If the opponent managed to circulate the ball to the weak side and the two forwards could not rotate across due to the distances, the weak side winger could

step up on the defender, always closing the outside-out passing line with the wingback.

In his last season at Dortmund, Klopp decided to experiment with high pressing using a 1-4-3-3 system with players in intermediate positions. As can be seen in Image 47, the wingers Reus (11) and Aubameyang (17) would position themselves between the central defender and fullback on each side and were responsible for squeezing the defenders. The players needed to press with a curved run, covering the passing line between the centerback and the fullback. The center forward, here Ciro Immobile (9), is man-marking the opposing defensive midfielder while the two attacking midfielders Mkhitaryan (10) and Gündoğan (8) step up to do the same with their counterparts.

In this example, the German coach's intention was to leave the fullbacks free so the opponent would be forced to either play an inside pass, skip a line, or perform a third-man maneuver with the fullback. This delivery would be very difficult for the opponent, due to the high density of players on the inside. In this way, favorable conditions were created for winning the ball in this zone.

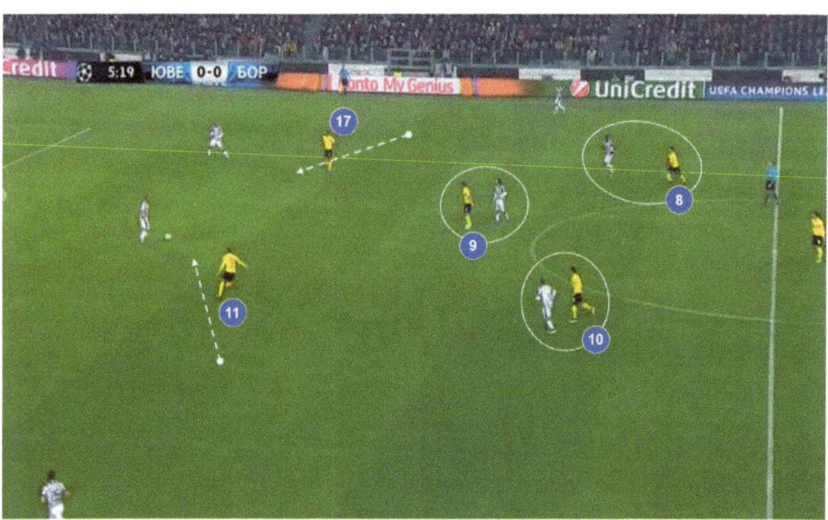

Image 47. Champions League quarter-final 2014/15: Juventus–Borussia Dortmund

Regardless of the system used or defensive principles being applied, if the opponent managed to escape the high press by playing short, the defenders would attempt to delay while all the players who had been overcome would attempt to recover and get back behind the ball. If the opponent played long, the players who were behind the ball would also drop back. However, Klopp's players would maintain their numerical superiorities in the defensive line and, as a general rule, would be able to win the duel and the second ball.

MEDIUM BLOCK

Defending in a medium block in a 1-4-4-2 was the most common behavior for Klopp's Borussia Dortmund. This block would constrict within a space of between 30 and 40 meters. It was a zonal operation based on shifting to cover the interior passing lines and directing the ball towards the wide channels, where progression would obviously be less dangerous and where they could look to win the ball. The priority for the first line of pressure was to prevent a pass inside to an opposing center midfielder. Initially, the two forwards would maintain positions at the same height in the central channel, allowing passes between the centerbacks and the circulation of the ball outside their defensive structure. The wingers would start in a position horizontal to the midfielders. In this way, the opponent's only option to build out short would be on the outside to a fullback dropping back.

If the opponent was unable to progress after several passes, one of the two forwards would take the initiative to steer the ball towards the outside, while the other would continue to mark the defensive midfielder. Often, the path taken to press the centerback in possession would be a simple straight-on run, and the inertia of the opponent's ball circulation would lead them to either pass or dribble the ball towards the outside.

With the ball in an outer channel, Klopp's team preferred to crowd the active playing zone and intensify their pressure. As can be seen in Image 48, the center forward Lewandowski (9) stays with the closest central defender to prevent a return pass. The attacking midfielder Reus (11) matches up with the opponent's defensive midfielder. The winger on the strong side, here Błaszczykowski (16), steps up on the opposing fullback while Piszczek (26), the fullback on that side, also moves up to guard against an outside-out pass. The remaining members of the two lines of four would shift, each occupying a channel while leaving the outer channel on the weak side free.

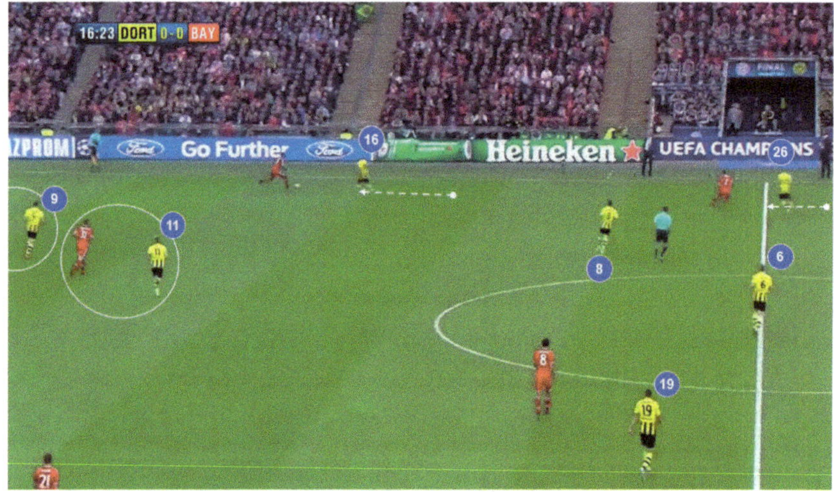

Image 48. Champions League final 2012/13: Borussia Dortmund–Bayern München

Klopp wanted his first line to provoke the mistake and the second line to recover the ball. In this situation, with the ball in the outer channel after having overcome the first line of pressure, the midfielder on the strong side would have a very important role. As Image 49 shows, in addition to closing the inside channel, the midfielder in the zone where the ball is, Gündoğan (8) in this example, would support the winger and the fullback to generate a 3-vs-2 superiority on the outside.

To ensure the block stayed narrow and maintained the correct distance between intervals, when the strong-side central midfielder would step up, the other central midfielder Bender (6) would shift to cover the inside passing lane, and the weak-side winger Großkreutz (19) would do the same thing in the central zone. In the event that the opponent managed to escape that 2-vs-3 situation and decided to progress on the strong side, Klopp had players nearby who could confront them and buy time for the midfielders to carry out a defensive switch of positions. If, on the other hand, the opponent decided to attack the weak side, there would still be time to carry out a quick defensive shift.

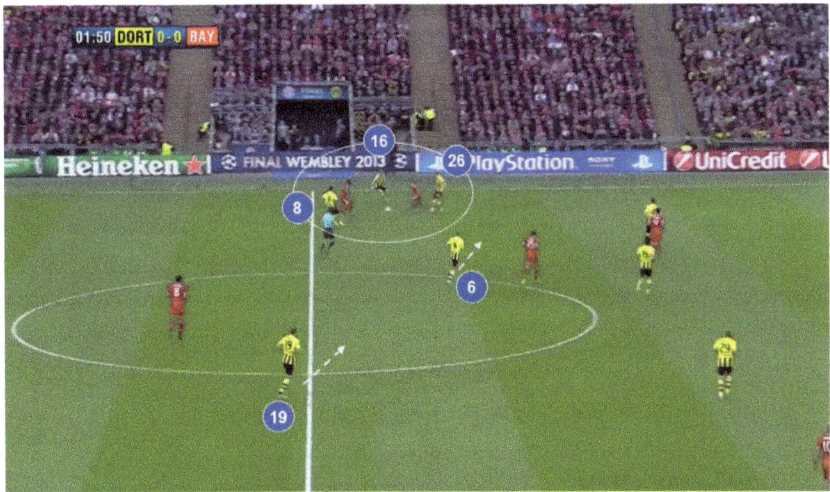

Image 49. Champions League final 2012/13: Borussia Dortmund–Bayern München

Along with the intense pressing on the outside, another key to effective defending in a medium block for Klopp's Borussia Dortmund was their aggressiveness when the ball was within the defensive structure. Image 50 shows several of the concepts applied by the German coach at that time. First, in this situation the defenders had to be narrow and would prioritize the protection of the interior zones, reducing the time and space available for the player in possession. Second, the ball carrier would not be allowed to turn and had to be pressured when he was facing his own goal, as the two midfielders Kehl (5) and Sahin (18) do here. Finally, when a player was overcome, he had to recover to help the line behind him with the purpose of generating a 2-vs-1 against the player in possession and preventing their progression. In this example, this behavior is carried out by the defensive midfielder Gündoğan (8) and the left attacking midfielder Sahin (18).

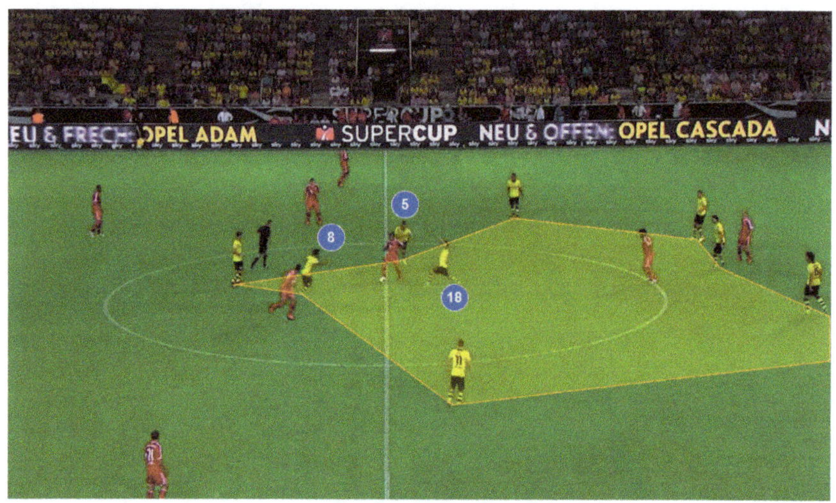

Image 50. German Super Cup 2013/14: Borussia Dortmund–
Bayern München

Faced with an outside-out pass, the fullbacks would pressure the opposing winger so that he could not turn. The defenders were constantly wacthing for the opposing center forward to drop down to support. As can be seen in Image 51, the closest central defender, here Hummels (15) on the left, has no problem leaving his zone and following his mark, aggressively looking for a chance to intercept the ball. However, it was vitally important for the fullback on that side, in this case Schmelzer (29), to move inside to cover him. If he does not perform this movement, as can be seen in Image 51, the opponents could take advantage of the very large hole that opens on the inside.

This aggressive manner of defending from the front allowed Klopp's Borussia Dortmund to win many balls in the middle third of the field. However, their moments of greatest vulnerability in midfield came when opposing teams managed to get past his midfield line or disorganized the defense by pulling players out of their zones.

Image 51. Champions League semi-final 2012/13: Real Madrid–
Borussia Dortmund

As shown in Image 52, if an opponent advances with the ball
unopposed, the defensive line would drop back and delay until
the opponent reached the top of the penalty area.

Image 52. Champions League semi-final 2012/13: Real Madrid–
Borussia Dortmund

In the event that an opponent would play the ball long, the defensive line would also be prepared to retreat.

LOW BLOCK

In a low block, Klopp used a 1-4-4-1-1 system that focused mainly on shifting from side to side, closing passing lines, and accumulating players in the active zone of play. As can be seen in Image 53 with the right midfielder Gündoğan (21), the ball was only pressed by the player from the midfield line who was in the same channel as the ball. Whenever the ball was switched to a different channel, the first player would recover his initial position and a teammate in the new channel would step up to apply pressure.

Whenever a midfielder would step up to a player in the central channel, as occurs in Image 53, the other central midfielder or the centerback on that side, Hummels (15) in this example, would move to provide cover in case the player who steps up was overcome by his opponent. If the player applying pressure was a defender, the three remaining members of the back line would get narrow to protect the central zone.

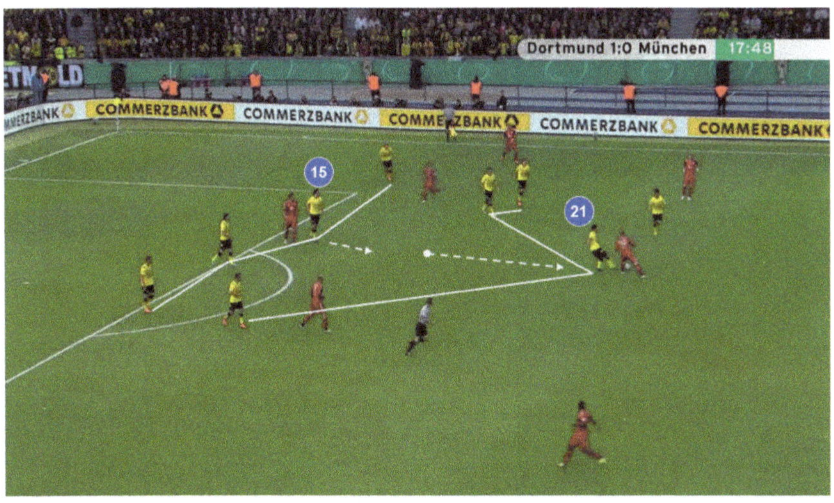

Image 53. German Cup final 2011/12: Borussia Dortmund–
Bayern München

In this system, the team released the center forward from direct defensive responsibilities so that he could remain disconnected from the defensive block and anticipate the offensive transition.

Just as he would do in a medium block, the attacking midfielder would use his position in the central channel to try and force the opponent to progress on the outside. At that time, Klopp always wanted to have a numerical superiority in the outer channels. As can be seen in Image 54, the winger on the strong side, in this case Błaszczykowski (16), would constantly support the fullback, here Piszczek (26). In this way they had a 2-vs-1 superiority against the opposing winger.

Image 54. Champions League semi-final 2012/13: Real Madrid–
Borussia Dortmund

As reflected in Image 55, when the opponent attacked with two players the midfielder of the strong side, who in this action is the left midfielder Bender (6), would shift to the outer channel to cover and support, creating a 3-vs-2 together with the winger and the fullback. The winger, here Großkreutz (19) on the left, would always try to defend from the front while the fullback, Schmelzer (29) in this action, would provide cover in case his teammate was overcome. The defensive midfielder was responsible for closing the passing line inside.

Image 55. Champions League semi-final 2012/13: Real Madrid–
Borussia Dortmund

In a low block, the fullbacks were instructed to always step up to the player in possession on the outside to block any potential crosses, maintaining a 3 + 1 structure along the last line. Consequently, they would need a teammate to cover them in case they were beaten in a 1-vs-1. Image 56 shows the preferred behavior: the winger on that side, in this case Mkhitaryan (10), drops down to position himself behind the fullback, here Piszczek (26), to provide cover.

Image 56. German Cup final 2013/14: Borussia Dortmund–
Bayern München

In the event that the winger was unable to get there, as can be seen in Image 57, the second option would be for the strong side midfielder, Sahin (18) in this situation, to provide cover.

Image 57. German Super Cup 2013/14: Borussia Dortmund–
Bayern München

Ultimately, if neither the winger nor the midfielder on that side could get there, it would be the centerback from that zone, in this case Subotić (4), who would take the risk of moving outside, as shown in Image 58.

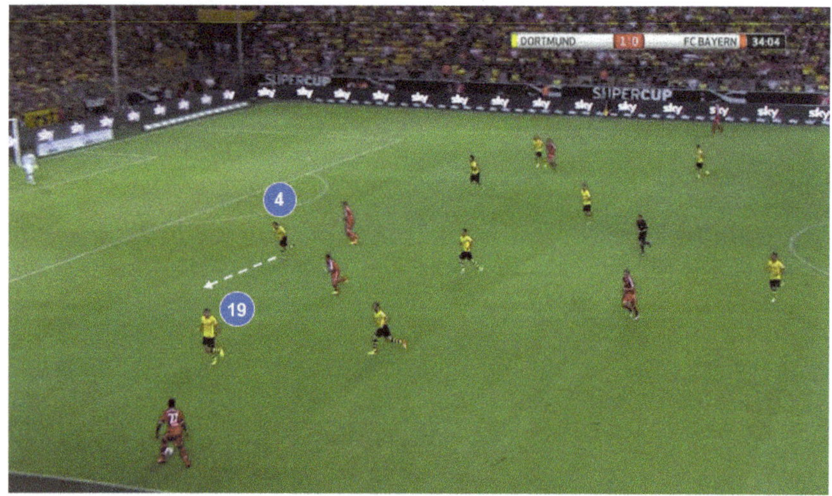

Image 58. German Super Cup 2013/14: Borussia Dortmund–
Bayern München

Crosses from the outside would be defended with a zonal 3 + 2 arrangement. As can be seen in Image 59, the fullback on the strong side, Schmelzer (29) on the left, goes outside to prevent the cross. Dortmund would distribute themselves within the penalty area as follows: the near side centerback Hummels (15) would cover the near post area; the far side centerback Subotić (4) would cover the penalty spot, and the weak side fullback Piszczek (26) would cover the far post. In front of them, as a general rule, would be two players: these could be the two defensive midfielders or, as observed in this case, the weak side winger Błaszczykowski (16) could also get to this area.

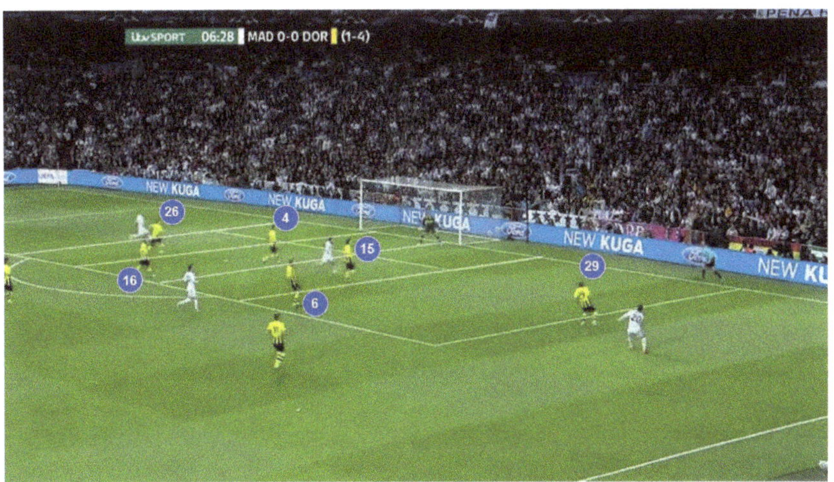

Image 59. Champions League semi-final 2012/13: Real Madrid–Borussia Dortmund

Defensive transition

Klopp's concept for this phase of the game stems from the German coaching school's traditional obsession with controlling the transitions. Influenced by Arrigo Sacchi, Ralf Rangnick, and Pep Guardiola among others, he began practicing *gegenpressing* tactics during his time at Borussia Dortmund.

This is a concept comparable to *la presión tras pérdida*, as it is known in Spanish. It consists of pressing in the active playing zone to regain possession immediately after losing the ball. It's a procedure that is carried out for a short period of time, and it starts from the front with the nearest players. Klopp took this philosophy and brought it one step further, trying to infuse it with a more offensive meaning.

When pressing after losing the ball, there can be different intentions. In Guardiola's Barcelona for example, its application was a form of protection and a way to dominate possession. The Spanish coach understood that the weakness of his team was its positional defense. Therefore, he carried out his pressing with the objective of avoiding the need to drop back to defend in his own half of the field. Upon recovering the ball his team would have even greater control of the game.

But another interpretation began to emerge, championed by Klopp, who intended to use pressing after losing the ball not only to prevent the opponent's progression, but also to prevent counterattacks, recover the ball, and launch his own counterattack immediately afterwards. As can be seen in the moments of the game diagram in Image 60, the German coach sought to use *gegenpressing* to turn a defensive transition into an offensive one.

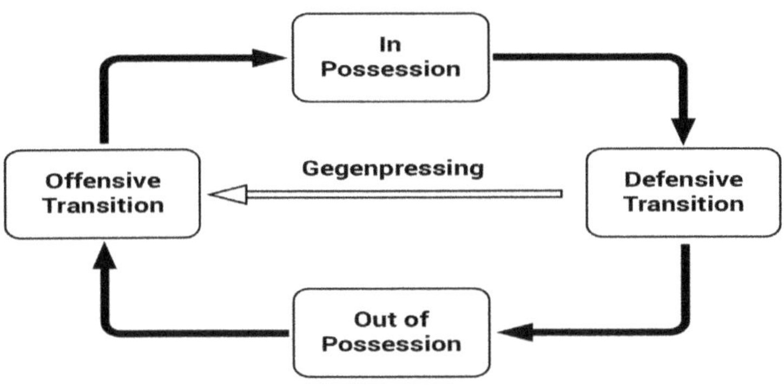

Image 60. G*egenpressing* during the moments of play. Author's
work

As Klopp commented in 2020: "There is no player in the world who can generate better scoring chances than *gegenpressing*." This statement illustrates how, after winning the ball in their defensive third, the opponent would be starting their counterattack without being positioned in their desired offensive structure, while Klopp's team still was. Thus, Klopp could counteract his opponent's transition by regaining possession during the opponent's organizational process, and by finding new spaces that did not previously exist when facing organized defenses. The resulting advantage would allow them to create clear-cut scoring situations with a single pass.

What set Klopp's way of pressing after losing the ball at Borussia Dortmund apart from the rest of the teams was his focus on hounding the ball. To this point, their structure in the opponent's half of the field during the offensive phase took on critical importance. As we have seen in Image 1, the inside position of the wingers guaranteed the accumulation of players in the active playing zone when the ball was lost. This would allow the nearest group of players to step up to the opponent in possession, compressing his space and time and generating the greatest amount of pressure possible to force bad decisions. *Gegenpressing* works best with teams that play with only one player in the outside channel. Teams that operate with several players on the wings have more problems doing this work correctly, because their players do not operate closely enough together.

As seen in Image 61, *gegenpressing* was executed by creating inverted triangles in 2 + 1 microstructures. Two players located in the upper vertices would exert pressure, as the attacking midfielder Reus (11) and the right midfielder Jojić (14) do here, while another player is positioned at the lower vertex to provide cover. Eventually, this action provoked a back-pass that was intercepted by the left winger positioned inside, Großkreutz (19), who launches the counterattack.

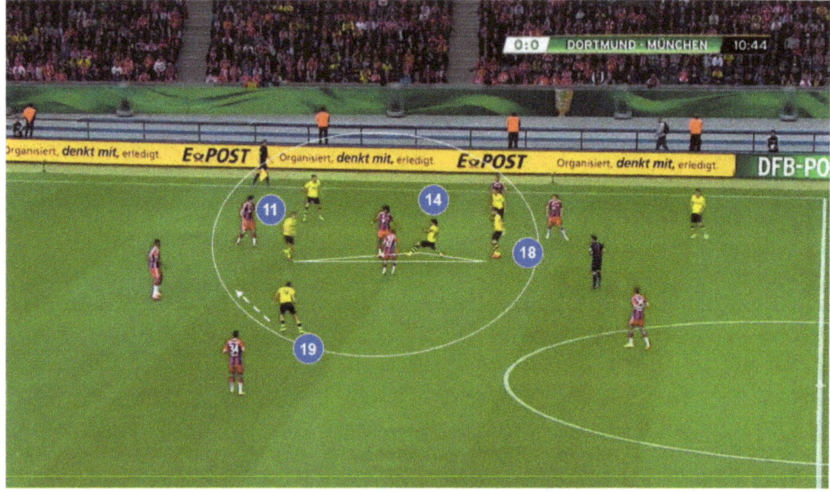

Image 61. German Cup Final 2013/14: Borussia Dortmund– Bayern München

Gegenpressing allows you to take the initiative and it means that the development of the game is governed by your own decisions instead of being at the mercy of the opponent, as happens when a team drops back defensively. Carrying it out requires a high capacity for anticipation. These actions are different from the organized pressing maneuvers in the defensive phase, and require constant adaptation to the changing contexts.

The notion has remained in the collective imagination that *gegenpressing* was one of the keys to the success of Klopp's Borussia Dortmund. However, in this period the theoretical idea was far removed from the practical application. Actually, at that time this strategy represented a new and emerging method, popularized by a winning team, but it was still far from being a consistent and effective formula as a whole.

Despite the physical demands required, the players internalized this change of behavior from being in possession to pressing after losing the ball. On most occasions, if Klopp's Borussia Dortmund managed to stop the counterattack through this type of pressing, they would recover the ball in areas far from the opponent's goal. For practical purposes it was still beneficial, because they now had the ball. But it was done in areas far from scoring areas and without open spaces to reach them directly. For this reason, Klopp could not fulfill the ultimate purpose of *gegenpressing*: to counterattack and create scoring situations immediately after recovering the ball.

This lack of effectiveness in application was due to the fact that on many occasions the nearby players instigated the loss of possession but did not recover the ball, something that would be accomplished by a teammate farther away. The pressure from the nearby players caused the player in possession to quickly play the ball long before it could be stolen. At that moment, the central defenders would be ready to anticipate and recover the ball to initiate a new positional attack in the opponent's half, as the left centerback Hummels (15) can be seen doing in Image 62.

Image 62. Bundesliga 2012/13: Bayern München–Borussia Dortmund

In the creation zone, Klopp's Borussia Dortmund would press after losing the ball in response to a failure to progress through vertical passes. These deliveries are more difficult and therefore have a lower chance of success. However, the other side of the coin is that more losses of the ball would be generated which therefore would generate more situations where pressure could be applied. Taking into account that his team was organized and mentally prepared to carry the strategy out, Klopp managed to turn this problem into an opportunity. This is exemplified by the action in Image 63: after an errant through pass, the two wingers Mkhitaryan (10) and Großkreutz (19) close in and press the player in possession, together with left fullback Erik Durm (37) and the left midfielder Oliver Kirch (21), to recover the ball.

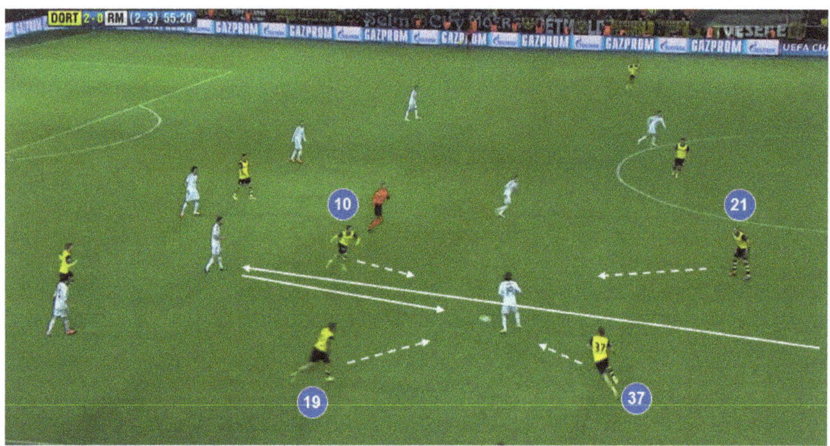

Image 63. Champions League quarter-final 2013/14: Borussia Dortmund–Real Madrid

In the finishing zone, the playing spaces are smaller. The attackers at Klopp's Borussia Dortmund were technically skilled and would constantly attempt wall passes, first-time passes, and dribbling actions. After losing possession as a result of these actions, they would put *gegenpressing* into practice. As Image 64 shows, the winger on the active side, here Reus (11), would immediately close down the player in possession to prevent him from turning. In this action, the German manages to steal the ball and the ensuing counterattack leads to a goal by the attacking midfielder Mkhitaryan (10).

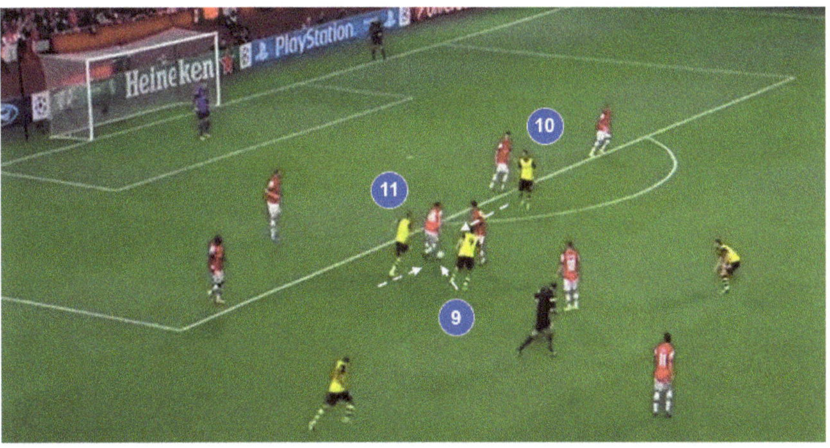

Image 64. Champions League group stage 2013/14: Arsenal–
Borussia Dortmund

Attacking into space also presents pressing situations like these after losing the ball: passes through the intervals behind the defense and switches of play to the weak side are both great opportunities for *gegenpressing*. In these contexts, the body position of the opposing defenders is often not correct and therefore they cannot clear the ball correctly. Image 65 reflects such an example: after an attempt to get behind the opposing fullback with a switch of play, the clearance is poor and the ball ends up on the edge of the penalty area. At that moment, both the left back Schmelzer (29) and the center forward Schieber (23) arrive to recover the ball and create a scoring chance.

Image 65. Champions League group stage 2012/13: Borussia Dortmund–Manchester City

Even so, pressing after losing the ball did not ensure that the team would regain possession. Whenever the opponent managed to overcome the pressing and get out of the recovery zone, Klopp's team would fall back. This was one of the moments of greatest vulnerability for his Borussia Dortmund: with the high position of the fullbacks in the offensive phase and the intervention of multiple players —including the midfielders— in the task of *gegenpressing*, the defensive line was left unprotected. The central defenders had to cover a lot of space at the back, and often had to go out wide in situations of numerical equality and even numerical inferiority. The only option they had to defend these situations was to delay in order to protect the central channel.

During his first seasons, defensive transitions were one of the main causes for the goals conceded by Klopp's Borussia Dortmund. The opponents found that the best way to counterattack was in the wide channels, behind the fullbacks. The German coach looked for ways to solve this problem.

First, he improved the ability of both fullbacks to immediately drop back. Second, he made the tactical decision to defend with three players to maintain superiority against one or two opposing forwards. As can be seen in Image 66, if both fullbacks were deployed in the attack then one of the midfielders, in this case Kirch (21), stayed back to defend with the central defenders Hummels (15) and Manuel Friedrich (2).

Image 66. Champions League quarter-final 2013/14: Borussia Dortmund—Real Madrid

If, on the other hand, both midfielders pushed up into the opponent's half of the field, as shown in Image 67, it would be the weak side fullback, here Piszczek (26) on the right, providing the defensive balance.

Image 67. Champions League quarter-final 2013/14: Borussia Dortmund–Real Madrid

Analysis of the phases of the game at Liverpool

Klopp's career at Liverpool bears many similarities to his time at Borussia Dortmund. When he signed for the club on October 8, 2015, he once again had the task of reviving a historic club that was going through a period of bad results.

Similarly, his time at Liverpool can also be distinguished by three stages. Klopp used the first two seasons (from 2015 to 2017) to adapt the fundamentals of his game model to the context of English football and rebuild the squad. One of the aspects to take into account in the team's successful resurrection is related to its high percentage of successful signings. In his second season he brought in fullback Trent Alexander-Arnold (from the academy), central defender Joel Matip, midfielder Georginio Wijnaldum, and forward Sadio Mané. He then completed his starting eleven by buying fullback Andrew Robertson, centerback Virgil van Dijk, midfielder Alex Oxlade-Chamberlain, and forward Mohamed Salah.

With this new squad, later joined by goalkeeper Alisson Becker and midfielder Fabinho, Klopp had assembled a dominant team capable of becoming the best in the world. In the following three years (from 2017 to 2020) his Liverpool reached two cup finals and earned Champions League and Premier League titles. In the 2020/21 season, injuries to key players resulted in a campaign with more modest results. That moment began a period of decline and subsequent rebuilding in a bid to return to the top.

Offensive phase

Systems

During his first season in 2015/16, Klopp was constantly searching for the system that would be most efficient and compatible with the characteristics of his players and his game model. Initially, he decided to continue with the 1-4-2-3-1 system with the wingers playing inside that had brought him so much success at Borussia Dortmund. He used this formation in 53.8% of the games during his first campaign (according to transfermarkt.com). He also experimented with playing without wingers and with two attacking midfielders in a 1-4-3-2-1. Eventually, he discarded this system because it made attacking the spaces within the opponent's back line too complicated.

While playing in the Europa League he continued to rely on the 1-4-2-3-1, but in the Premier League he began to experiment with systems using a single defensive midfielder, such as the 1-4-3-3 and its variant the 1-4-1-4-1. In this way, he had five players (the three forwards plus the two attacking midfielders) to deploy in the attack, occupying the five channels more rationally.

Since the 2016/17 season, the 1-4-3-3 system has become the basic scheme in the offensive phase. While in 2015/16 Klopp only used it in 23% of the games, in the following five campaigns it has been his primary system, used 82% of the time (according to transfermarkt.com). As can be seen in Image 68, the 1-4-3-3 system allows two players to occupy each channel at different heights. The starting point for their deployment is: the fullbacks, in this case Robertson (26) and Joe Gomez (12), and the wingers Oxlade-Chamberlain (15) and Salah (11) stay wide; the centerbacks Van Dijk (4) and Matip (32) and the attacking midfielders James Milner (7) and Jordan Henderson (14), position themselves in the interior channels; and the defensive midfielder Fabinho (3) and the center forward Mané (10) occupy the central channel. The characteristics of this system allow for the creation of triangles among all the nearby players in order to progress in different relationships with vertical, horizontal, diagonal, and short passes as well as third-man actions.

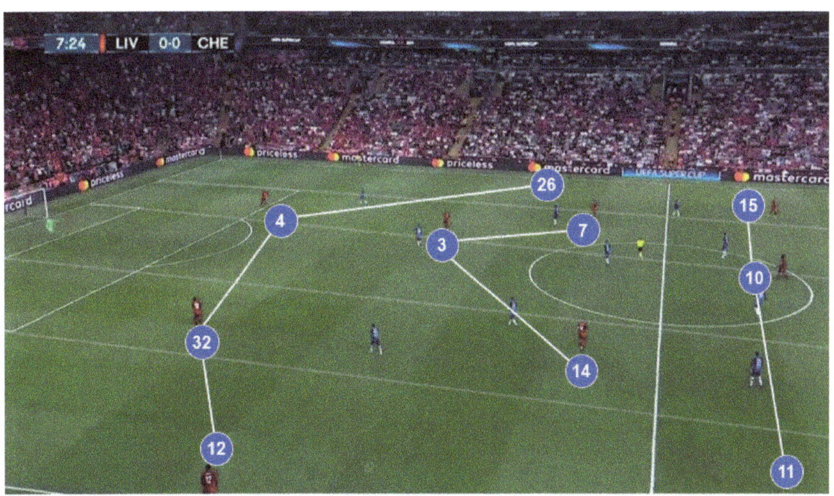

Image 68. European Super Cup 2019/20: Liverpool–Chelsea

But in the opponent's half of the field, by pushing the fullbacks up and moving the off-footed wingers inside, the 1-4-3-3 system becomes a 1-2-5-3. As Image 69 shows, this spatial distribution has six players accumulated inside while 2 players attack in the width. In general, it's the fullbacks who stay wide, although it can also be the wingers. In this way they force the opposing defenses to narrow and protect the central zone, which frees up space on the outside. By having a wide player in each outside channel, both positioned at a height between the opponent's defensive and midfield lines, Klopp's team always maintains positional superiority on the weak side. By keeping a player on the weak side, Liverpool can usually get on the ball there faster than the opponent can shift.

In the application of Klopp's game model at Liverpool, the players are part of a dynamic and adaptive system that encourages positional flexibility. As long as the spatial structure is respected, a non-negotiable requirement for carrying out his specific principles, the offensive players in the creation and finishing zones are given a certain amount of freedom to swap their positions in accordance with how they anticipate the action.

Image 69. Champions League final 2017/18: Real Madrid–
Liverpool

Organized attack

STARTING ZONE

Klopp's idiosyncrasy demands that the ball spends most of its time in the opponent's half of the field. During the first six seasons his Liverpool team had possession in the first third of the pitch just 23.5% of the time (according to transfermarkt.com). Following the same rationale as his buildout with four defenders at Borussia Dortmund, in England Klopp places his centerbacks in the interior channels (channels 2 and 4).

Despite this, Liverpool's squad in the 2015/16 campaign did not have defenders with sufficient technical quality on the ball to take responsibility for initiating short buildouts. As a solution, when Klopp built out with three players he used both defensive midfielders to generate superiorities of 3 + 1 in a 4-vs-2 or 4-vs-1 at the start. Most of the first lines of defensive pressure he faced that season were made up of two players, both horizontally and vertically, to steer the ball to one side.

As can be seen in Image 70, one of the mechanisms to form the buildout shape with three in the back was to push a center midfielder, in this case Milner (7), out wide. Dejan Lovren was the squad's best centerback during the buildout in the 2015/16 season, so normally the midfielder would get wide on the opposite side from the Croatian. In this example the fullback on the strong moves up while Lovren (6), the centerback on the far side, moves wide to increase the distances the opposing forwards are forced to defend. The other midfielder, here Emre Can (23), positions himself behind the opponent's first line to fix those players.

As Image 70 shows, if the opponent's first line of pressure was positioned horizontally, it would force the two forwards to remain narrow to protect the central channel, since both could be overcome with a single vertical pass. On the other hand, if the opposing attackers defend vertically, Liverpool's defensive midfielder would fix his pair of opponents, which allowed the creation of a 3-vs-1 against the forward who stepped up to press. If the opponent's first line of pressure was passive, Klopp's team would simply circulate the ball to the side where their midfielder had gone out wide.

Once the 3 + 1 numerical superiority was generated as a 4-vs-2, the midfielder who went out wide, here Milner (7), could run with the ball through the inside channel. It's important that he did not drop down too far (that is: when he received the ball he needed to be in a position to immediately overcome the opponent's first line) so that a player from the second line would have to step up to pressure him. In this example he provokes the opponent marking the fullback, here Mkhitaryan (10), to move inside; either because he would be fixed by the player running with the ball or because he must cover the interior space behind the teammate stepping up to pressure. By forcing that situation, Milner (7) creates a passing line with the left back that allows the team to progress through the outside channel.

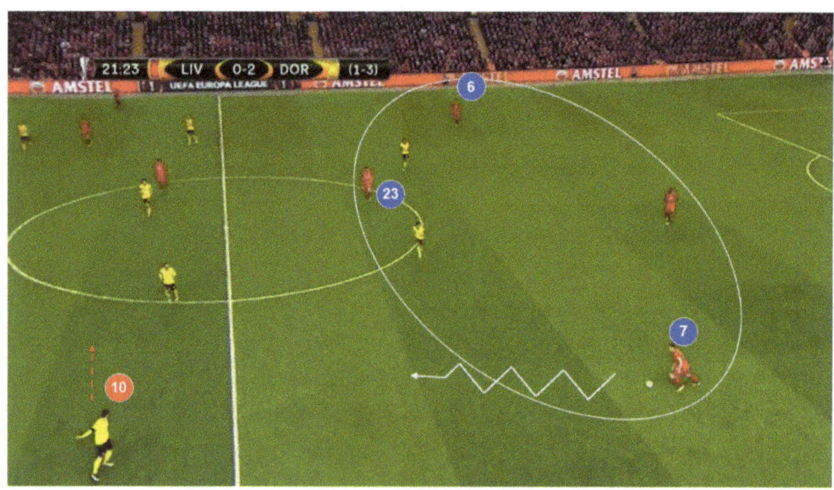

Image 70. Europa League quarter-final 2015/16: Liverpool–
Borussia Dortmund

The second buildout mechanism consisted of forming a line of three by dropping one of the midfielders between the centerbacks. As can be seen in Image 71, a midfielder, in this case Can (23), would drop down at the same moment that the central defenders Lovren (6) and Mamadou Sakho (17) open up to increase the distances that must be defended. By circulating the ball with a switch of play from one side to the other, Liverpool would play in superiority with the objective of turning one of the two wide players in the line of three into a free man who could escape the pressure through an outside channel. If they couldn't progress with that 3 + 1 numerical advantage, the midfielder in front of the ball could also move out wide to help the buildout from the outside.

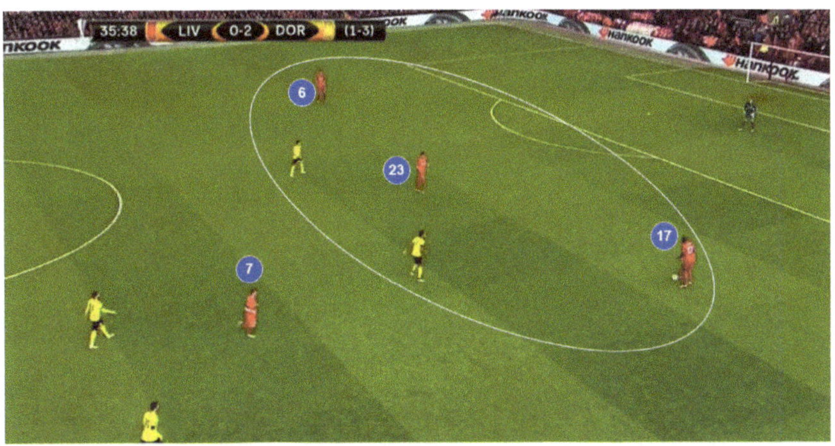

Image 71. Europa League quarter-finals 2015/16: Liverpool–
Borussia Dortmund

As can be seen in Image 72, if the two players in the opponent's first line of pressure were too far from each other horizontally, the midfielder located between the central defenders, who in this situation is Can (23), could advance by running between them with the ball. By eliminating this first defensive barrier with a drive through the central channel, the second line is now forced to get narrower inside, freeing up the fullbacks to progress on the outside.

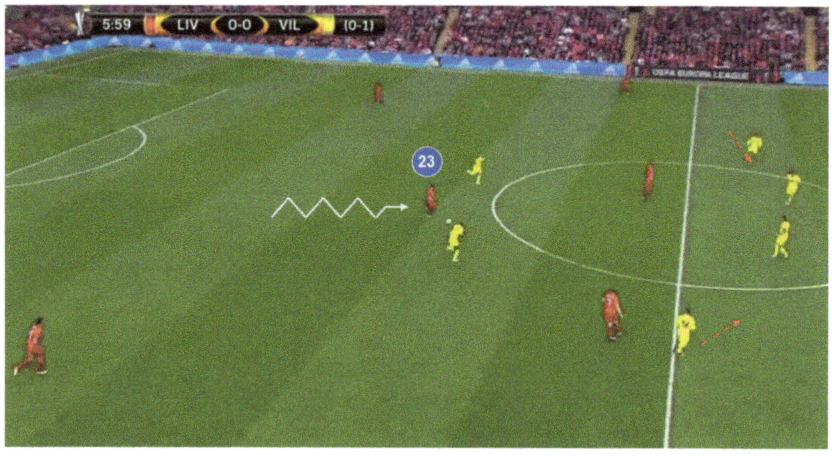

Image 72. Europa League semi-finals 2015/16: Liverpool–
Villarreal

With the change of system to a 1-4-3-3 from the 2016/17 season onwards, Klopp has substantially modified the mechanisms used in the starting zone, building out with a line of four players. In his holistic view of the sport, he believes that the players furthest away from the ball play a fundamental role in this phase. As Image 73 shows, the three forwards, who pose a great threat to the open space behind the opponents, have the function of fixing the defenders on the back line, positioning themselves within the visual field of the four defenders and within their intervals. Hardly any opponent has the courage to leave a 3-vs-3 on their back line. Consequently, Liverpool always manages to have an 8-vs-6 numerical superiority in their own half of the field. Without that permanent attacking threat there could be no fixing of defenders in the back line, and therefore no superiority in their own half.

Image 73. Champions League final 2018/19: Tottenham–
Liverpool

Based on this numerical superiority, and based on the premise that opponents will always prioritize defending the central channel, Klopp's team has developed several mechanisms to progress to the opposite half of the field as quickly as possible, with a fundamental concept being that of the third man. The German coach's Liverpool prefers to advance on the outside. During his first six seasons, 71.8% of the attacks went through the flanks: 35.4% from the left and 36.4% from the right (according to whoscored.com).

Against opponents who press with a single forward in the front line who positions himself between the centerbacks to steer the ball towards one of the wings (in the 1-4-2-3-1, 1-4-4-1-1, or 1-3-4-2-1 systems), Klopp's solution is to build out through a fullback (either directly or through a third man action). As can be seen in Image 74 the defensive midfielder, here Henderson (14), frequently makes movements to occupy the free space generated when the opponents step up. In these scenarios the pivot can act as a third man with the right back Nathaniel Clyne (2), as he does in this example. By receiving the ball unmarked, the midfielder can also turn and progress directly.

Image 74. Premier League 2016/17: Liverpool–Tottenham

As Image 75 shows, against rivals organized with two strikers in a 1-4-4-2 formation with horizontal lines, Klopp's players generate superiority with a 4-vs-2 in a diamond shape consisting of the goalkeeper, in this case Loris Karius (1), two center backs playing wide, and the defensive midfielder Henderson (14), who operates in the interval behind and between the two forwards. The German coach tries to keep his fullbacks at a certain height to fix the opposing wingers and to separate the opponent's first line from the second, making the total playing area larger. In this way, the pivot has enough time and space to receive the ball and turn as the free player behind the attackers.

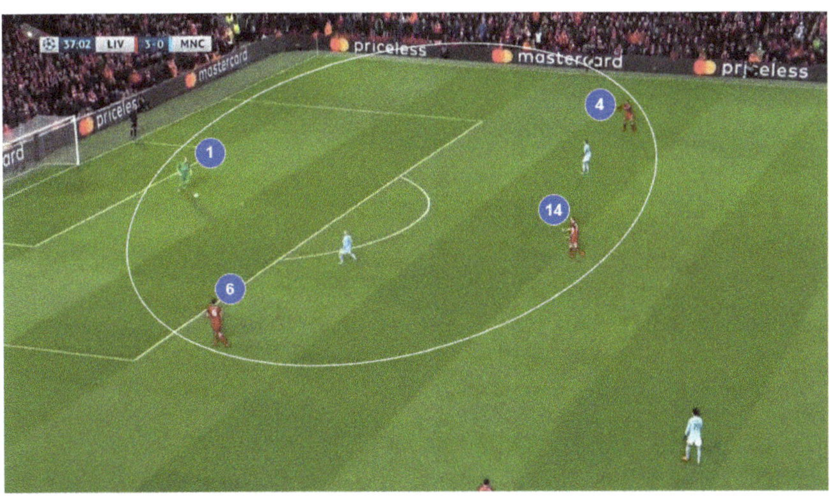

Image 75. Champions League quarter-final 2017/18: Liverpool–
Manchester City

Against opponents who press with two forwards and mark the defensive midfielder (in the 1-4-4-2 diamond or 1-4-1-3-2 systems), the free man in numerical superiority can be found on the weak side. As can be seen in Image 76, after luring the forwards to step up by playing a pass backwards to the goalkeeper, Liverpool seeks to generate a 3-vs-1 superiority against the opponent's attacking midfielder, who in this situation is Yacine Brahimi (8). The weak side attacking midfielder, here Wijnaldum (5), drops down to act as a short passing option within the field of vision of the opposing attacking midfielder Brahimi (8), while the right centerback Matip (32) and right back Alexander-Arnold (66) stay wide. In this way, the opposing midfielder Brahimi (8) must make a decision as to whether to step up to one of the three opponents, and as a result the goalkeeper Alisson (13) switches play to one of the free men.

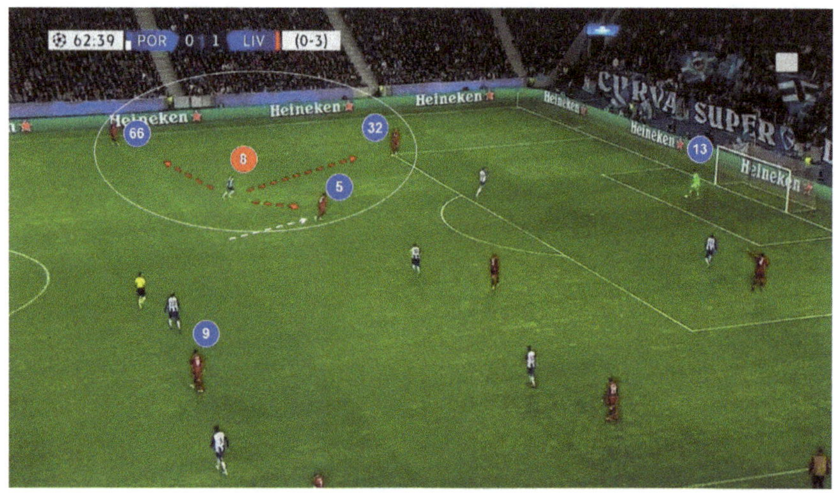

Image 76. Champions League quarter-final 2018/19: Oporto–
Liverpool

Against opponents playing with systems with three players in the front row, the intention is to lure the opponents inside to turn the fullbacks into free men. Image 77 reflects this behavior against a rival who is pressing high in a 1-4-3-3. Again, one of the attacking midfielders, in this case Wijnaldum (5), drops down to generate a numerical superiority of 2-vs-1 with the defensive midfielder, here Fabinho (3), against the center forward in the central channel. In this way, Liverpool seeks to draw the opponent to one side and build out through the other, causing one of the opposing wingers to go inside and generating space and time for the central defender on his side to progress on the outside. If the opponent does not make that decision, one of the two players in the numerical advantage has the option of running inside with the ball.

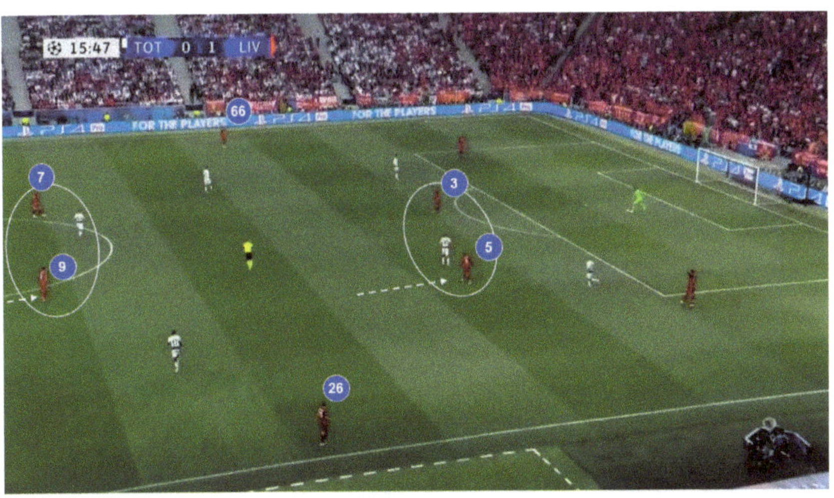

Image 77. Champions League final 2018/19: Tottenham–
Liverpool

In order to preserve the three-player structure in the second line, when one of the interior players drops down, the center forward, who in this action is Firmino (9), does the same. What this player can do in these situations is both offer a passing line at a different height, as shown in Image 76, and generate another 2-vs-1 numerical superiority against the opposing defensive midfielder in the central channel with the other inside player, who in this situation is Milner (7), as can be seen in Image 77.

Against systems with five players in the back line (such as the 1-5-3-2 or 1-5-2-2-1), Klopp's Liverpool looks to build out on the wing. As Image 78 shows, the right winger Salah (11) fixes the wingback so that he cannot pressure on the outside. Because the right back Alexander-Arnold (66) is positioned at a medium height, this allows him to receive the ball from the centerback and drive forward with the entire outside channel free. In the event that the wingback decides to pressure the him, his height and positioning affords him the space and time to control the ball and play it into the path of the winger, behind the back of the opponent who steps up.

Image 78. Champions League group stage 2020/21: Atalanta–
Liverpool

A major buildout mechanism for Klopp's Liverpool is to use the third man concept and then make a vertical pass to a more advanced line. This automatism allows them to progress quickly (with two or three passes and two or three touches of the ball) and switch channels, using diagonal or wall passes thanks to the triangular structures provided by the 1-4-3-3 system.

Depending on their spatial relationships with the player in possession, Klopp's team has established four different buildout patterns: two for combining with nearby players and another two for combining with more distant ones. These actions will be adapted to the problems posed by each individual game situation.

First, Liverpool uses the inside-out-in passing sequence. As can be seen in Image 79, the defensive midfielder Fabinho (3) acts as the third man on the next line to play a pass outside to the fullback on the side where the ball is, in this case Alexander-Arnold (66). Next, this player threads a vertical pass inside. In this example the first two passes serve to draw opponents to the outer channels (where most teams seek to win the ball when they press high), and it's the third pass that really overcomes the pressure.

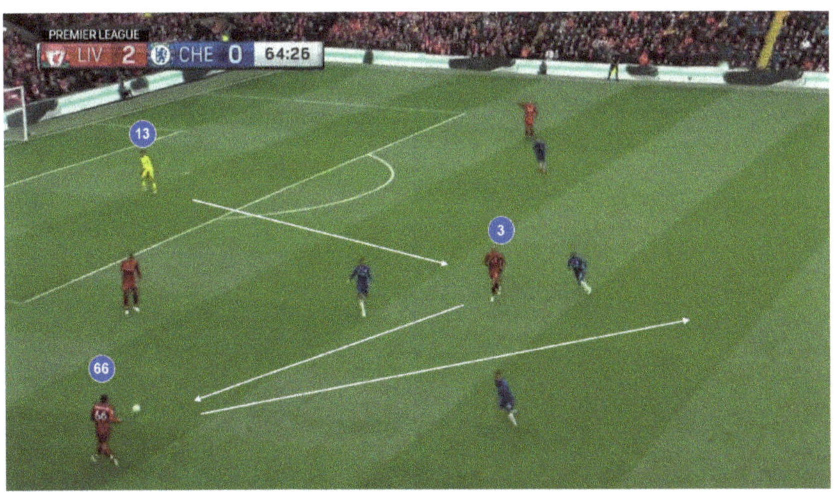

Image 79. Premier League 2018/19: Liverpool–Chelsea

Second, they can apply an outside-inside-out passing sequence, as can be seen in Image 80. In these situations the fullback on the active side, who in the example is Alexander-Arnold (66) on the right, operates as the third man on the outside to find the defensive midfielder Fabinho (3) on the inside after he makes a supporting movement behind the opposing striker who has stepped up. The pivot then plays the ball out wide again to the attacking midfielder or winger. In this case, the first pass serves to attract opponents to the outside and it's the second pass that effectively breaks the pressure.

Image 80. Champions League group stage 2019/20: Liverpool–
Red Bull Salzburg

A third variant is to find a more distant third man in the
same channel, as shown in Image 81. In this example the right
centerback Lovren (6) threads a vertical pass within the interior
channel directly to Salah (11), the winger on his side. In this
situation the first pass breaks the pressure and skips the midfield
line, and the winger lays the ball off to put the interior player, the
right attacking midfielder Wijnaldum (5), in a forward-facing
position with the ball at his feet. If the winger's marker follows
him in this scenario, there is a chance that the player receiving
the ball can pass into the newly created space to a fourth man
(usually the center forward) dismarking from the inside-out.

Image 81. Champions League final 2017/18: Real Madrid–
Liverpool

A fourth option is to build out with a distant third man in a different channel, as can be seen in Image 82. After playing through the outside channel with the left fullback, in this case Alberto Moreno (18), this player delivers a long pass to the center forward Firmino (9), who is dropping back in the interior channel to act as the third man. If this player's marker steps up, which will open up space along the back line, he can lay the ball off to the nearby attacking midfielder Wijnaldum (5), who can play the next pass deep and into space for a fourth man running in behind. In this example the run is executed by the left winger Mané (19), but it can also be carried out by the outside attacker on the weak side.

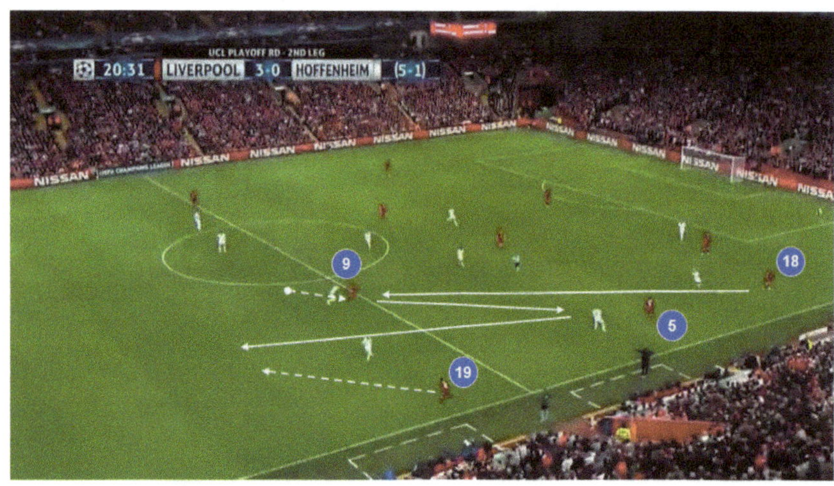

Image 82. Champions League qualifying round 2017/18:
Liverpool–Hoffenheim

In every season, Klopp's Liverpool have completed more short passes per game than in the previous year. In the 2020/21 campaign (591) they finished with an average of 131 more short passes per game than in Klopp's first season in 2015/16 (460). Despite this, the German's team excels at managing direct play and aerial duels, a tactic he will use when faced with high pressing or in situations where the team cannot progress with short passes. None of the three strikers who have been the most influential throughout this cycle, Salah, Firmino, or Mané, are tall. However, they are all very good at using their bodies to win second balls and do not usually shy away from aerial duels.

As was the case at Borussia Dortmund, Klopp is capable of building teams that are very effective at winning second balls. The Stuttgart-born coach has made his players appreciate the importance of winning these actions in order to start attacks in the opponent's half of the field. Therefore whenever an aerial duel occurs, the Liverpool players will surround the area where the ball will drop and quickly activate themselves if the ball is not won. This behavior is demonstarted by the center forward Firmino (9) and the right attacking midfielder Oxlade-Chamberlain (21) in Image 83.

Image 83. Premier League 2017/18: Liverpool–Manchester City

Klopp's team also has a mechanism to play directly from the starting zone into the space behind the opponent's defense. If the buildout is carried out through a fullback and the winger on the same side is positioned in the interior channel, as seen in Image 84, the attacker on that wing, who in this maneuver is Salah (11), makes an inside-out dismark, behind the opposing fullback and into the interval between the centerback and fullback. Very often, this type of action develops on the right side, through Alexander-Arnold and Salah.

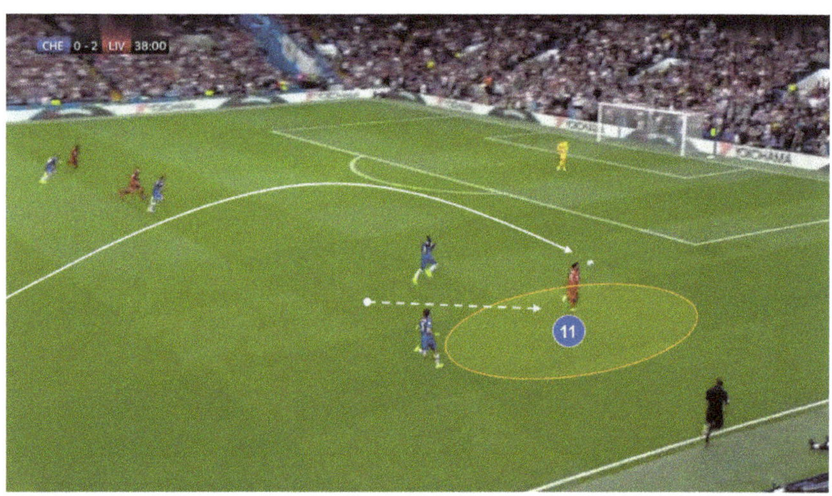

Image 84. Premier League 2019/20: Chelsea–Liverpool

CREATION ZONE

As we have seen, Klopp's Liverpool pushes his fullbacks up the field a lot, forming a 1-2-5-3 spatial arrangement. This structure makes it possible to form three triangles. On the sides, the triangles are made up of the fullback, the attacking midfielder, and the winger, and are intended to generate 3-vs-2 superiorities out wide. As can be seen in Image 85, the conventional spatial organization consists of having one player in the outer channel —in this case the left back, Robertson (26)— and two others at different heights in the inside channel here, the left attacking midfielder Milner (7) and the left winger Mané (10).

In principal, this structure can lead to the center forward becoming isolated. However, because Klopp has players with high levels of mobility and good technique, this is not a problem. The best example is Firmino (9): his technical-tactical nature instinctively allows him to generate synergies with his teammates around the ball, and the German coach gives him the autonomy to drop down to help generate superiorities in the front line. The players who fulfill this function can make movements along the horizontal axis, can form part of the outer triangles, or operate on the vertical axis to generate an advantage in the middle of the field, together with the three midfielders.

Another triangle is formed in the central channel between the defensive midfielder and the two central defenders. By dominating that space, Klopp ensures that his team always has a superiority of three players against the opponent's first line of pressure. In this way, if they are unable to progress, Liverpool can quickly switch the direction of play with one or two touches and attack the weak side while the opponent is shifting. In addition, this is a means of providing defensive balance if the ball is lost.

Image 85. European Super Cup 2019/20: Liverpool–Chelsea

To progress in the creation zone, Klopp's Liverpool looks to generate numerical superiorities with at least two players more than their opponents have. The most common way of doing this is to create 4-vs-1 or 4-vs-2 advantages in a diamond shape with an attacking midfielder getting wide, with three players

in front of the opponent's first line of pressure and one player behind it. Image 86 shows an example of this action, with the right attacking midfielder Henderson (14) positioned alongside the central defenders while the defensive midfielder Fabinho (3) is located behind the first opponent. In this situation, the team builds out on the outside with a deep pass to the high fullback (located behind the opponent's second line).

Image 86. European Super Cup 2019/20: Liverpool–Chelsea

Sometimes Liverpool generate a superiority with four players, with a fullback dropping down (at the height of the opponent's second line). Against opponents with three players in the front line, as can be seen in Image 87, both mechanisms combine to maintain the two player numerical advantage, in a 5-vs-3 situation. The attacking midfielder on the side where the ball is, here Wijnaldum (5), moves wide while the left back Robertson (26) does not push up too far, in order to help in the buildout.

Image 87. Premier League 2018/19: Tottenham–Liverpool

When the wingers move inside, this becomes an invitation for the fullbacks to push forward. In this situation, another progression mechanism consists of a deep pass from a central defender to an outside defender positioned high in the opponent's half of the field, which allows the team to instantly overcome two lines of pressure. As can be seen in Image 88, the attacking midfielder closest to the ball, in this case Naby Keïta (8) on the right, occupies the winger's normal space in the interior zone, causing the opposing winger, here James Maddison (10), to hesitate in blocking the passing line between the centerback and the fullback, since there is also an inside passsing threat. The central defender Gómez (12) will react according to the movement of the opponent on the active wing. If the opponent gets narrow, as happens in this example, this defender can pass to the high fullback, Alexander-Arnold (66) on this occasion. If the opponent goes wide, the center back Gómez (12) can play inside to the attacking midfielder Keïta (8).

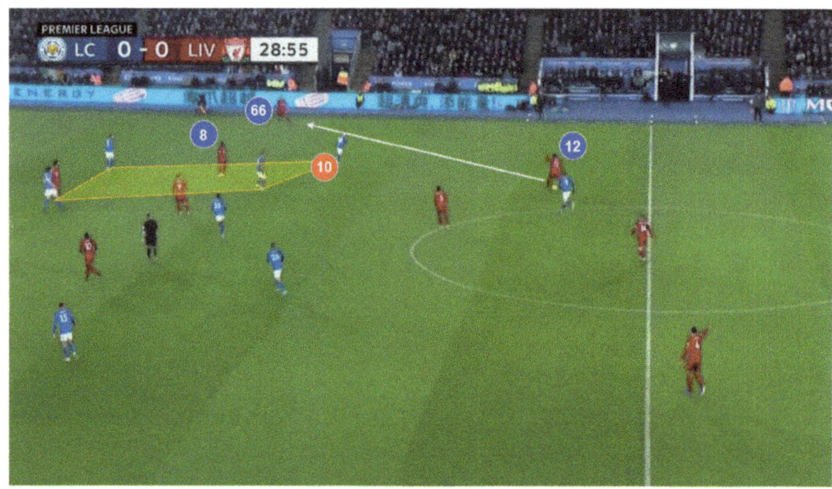

Image 88. Premier League 2019/20: Leicester–Liverpool

As we have seen, the standard setup for Klopp's Liverpool in the opponent's half of the field is to position the fullback wide and the winger inside. But in the 2018/19 season the German coach introduced the variant that can be seen in Image 89: on the right side, the wide players would often alternate their positions and the winger, usually Salah (11), would make himself available in the outside channel while the fullback, usually Alexander-Arnold (66), would position himself within the inside channel. The Egyptian is a player who exploits space with tremendous efficiency, but he also generates a lot of danger with the ball at his feet. As Klopp uses off-footed wingers, in these situations he's looking for Salah to receive the ball and drive inside, where he has the technical ability to beat players by dribbling at them 1-vs-1 or by playing wall passes with a teammate.

Image 89. Premier League 2019/20: Leicester–Liverpool

One of Klopp's most repeated patterns at Liverpool for attacking medium blocks from the creation zone is the switch of play. If the buildout occurs on one side, this area serves as the launch pad to change the direction of the attack and reach the finishing zone through the opposite side. If no progression can be made after a sequence of passes along the back line, as in Image 90, the central defender on the strong side, here the left centerback Rhys Williams (46), looks to switch the play diagonally to the free man on the weak side, in this case the right back Alexander-Arnold (66).

Image 90. Premier League 2020/21: Manchester United–
Liverpool

However, the most common way to switch play is through a central midfielder. One of the fundamental principles in the offensive phase of Klopp's Liverpool is to attack free spaces: attract players to one side of the field in order to attack on the opposite side. First, his team accumulates passes on the flank and creates a density of players in the central channel. In this way they draw the block's attention and force them to shift, which frees up the outer channel on the weak side. For this automation to work, two tactical aspects are essential: keeping two players out wide and controlling space at the "base" (the space between the opposing center forwards and midfielders). With their distribution of players in the opponent's half of the field, Klopp's team fulfills both requirements.

As can be seen in Image 91, the fullbacks, in this case Robertson (26) and Alexander-Arnold (66), occupy the wings as both the starting point and terminus of the action. The base must always be occupied, either with the defensive midfielder alone or, as in this situation, with the support of a player like the right attacking midfielder Henderson (14), in order to switch play quickly and effectively.

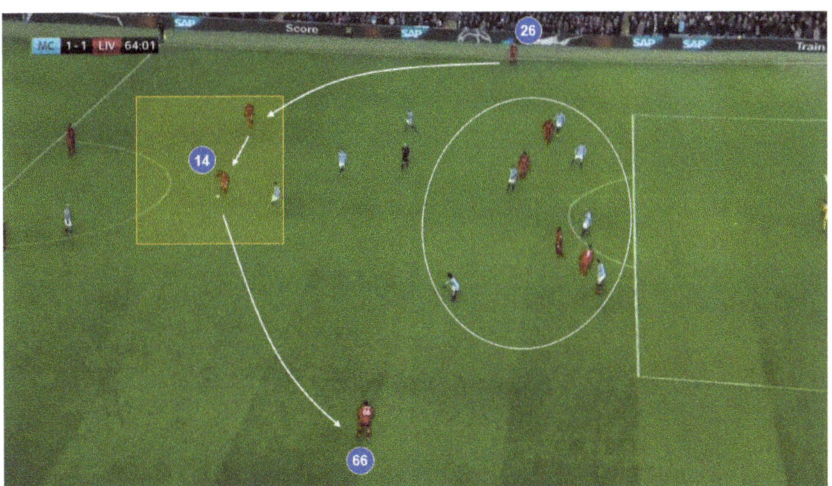

Image 91. Premier League 2018/19: Manchester City–Liverpool

Since the 2018/19 season, these types of diagonal switches of play to the free man on the weak side have evolved: they are no longer only executed by the central defenders, but are now also executed directly from fullback to fullback. Image 92 demonstrates this with the players who usually fulfill this function; Alexander-Arnold (66) and Robertson (26). In this way, Klopp's Liverpool have moved a step further in their quest to optimize their ideals of quick progression. Now they no longer require an intermediate pass to get the ball from one side to the other.

With these switches of play between the fullbacks, the team has the ability to dominate the entire width of the active playing area and to more efficiently exploit the shifting of their opponents. Once the switch is completed, the first thing the player receiving the ball will do is move forward to gain territory and attack the opponent's back line. Failing that, if the defense manages to fall back, Liverpool has at least forced their opponent into the final third of the field.

Image 92. Premier League 2019/20: Liverpool–Manchester City

Within the 1-4-3-3 or 1-2-5-3 systems, the spatial relationships between the three midfielders play a critical role when progressing with the ball. Depending on the game situation, they alternate different rotations in an unpredictable manner. The starting position is always in the shape of a "V". As can be seen in Image 93, the two attacking midfielders, in this case Wijnaldum (5) and Oxlade-Chamberlain (15), are positioned higher up in the interior channels than the defensive midfielder Henderson (14), who remains in the central channel. When the ball is in the middle of the field, the movements of the attacking midfielders are mainly vertical. They can drop down a bit to occupy the spaces next to the opposing midfielders, as shown in Image 93, or move further forward in the interior zones, as shown in Image 94.

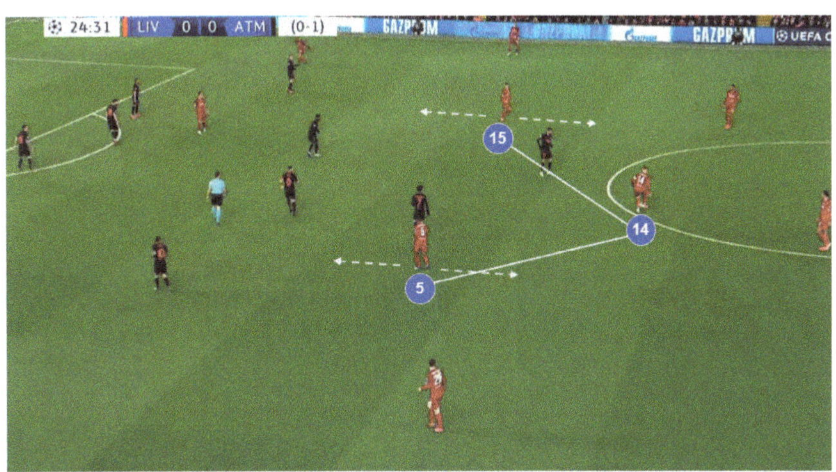

Image 93. Champions League quarter-final 2019/20: Liverpool–
Atlético de Madrid

In the event that an attacking midfielder receives the ball
in one of these zones, as shown in Image 94 with the right
attacking midfielder (temporarily positioned on the left) Oxlade-
Chamberlain (21), this player controls the ball with his body
positioned so that in two touches, with a reception and a pass, he
is able to play deep and attack the opponent's back line. Image
94 shows how this is a very effective mechanism for progressing
rapidly against opponents who defend in a medium block.

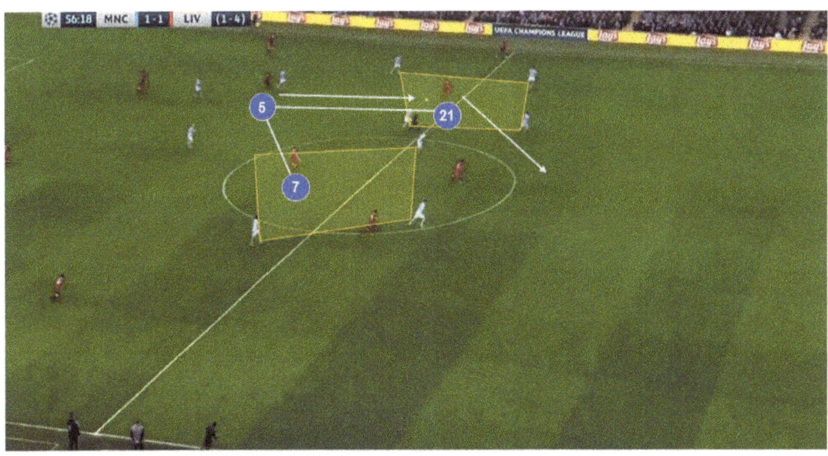

Image 94. Champions League quarter-final 2017/18: Manchester
City–Liverpool

If the defensive midfielder drops down in an inside channel as an option to receive the ball and switch play, the attacking midfielder on the weak side also drops down to open up a horizontal passing lane with the pivot. As can be seen in Image 95, this movement results in an "L" shaped formation, with the attacking midfielder on the strong side, in this case Henderson (14) on the right, higher up in the same channel as the defensive midfielder Fabinho (3), while the left attacking midfielder on the weak side, here Keïta (8), is on the same horizontal axis as the pivot.

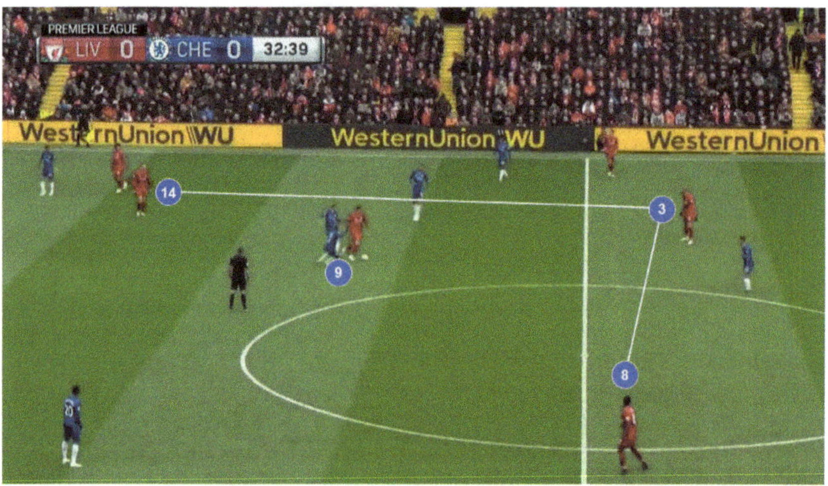

Image 95. Premier League 2018/19: Liverpool–Chelsea

In situations as in Image 96 where the attacking midfielder on the active side, in this case Curtis Jones (17) on the left, drops down and moves out wide, the defensive midfielder Wijnaldum (5) moves up to get behind the opponent's first line of pressure and form a diagonal line across the pitch with Thiago (6), the right attacking midfielder on the weak side, who holds his position. If the opponent's wide player blocks the outside pass between the attacking midfielder and fullback or the center midfielders drop too much, the pivot Wijnaldum (5) serves as a passing option to link with the other midfielder Thiago (6).

Image 96. Premier League 2020/21: Liverpool–Manchester City

During the first two seasons (from 2015 to 2017), there were frequent rotations within the fullback-attacking midfielder-winger triangle. As can be seen in Image 97, three movements would occur simultaneously: the fullback on the active side, who in this case is the left back Moreno (18), would move up on the outside; the winger Firmino (9) would move inside, and the attacking midfielder Philippe Coutinho (10) would drop down and profile his body to receive the ball facing forward. With these movements, the ball would reach one of the players with the greatest ability to play vertically. At the same time, this would generate uncertainty about who to mark among the opponent's two outside players, creating free spaces that could be occupied.

Image 97. Premier League 2015/16: Liverpool–Everton

Starting with the 2018/19 season, against medium blocks with narrow midfield lines that prioritized defending the interior spaces, Klopp's Liverpool has used another mechanism for progression. This mechanism consists of a supporting movement from the attacking midfielder on the active side, who in Image 98 is the left midfielder Milner (7), into the outside channel in front of the the left fullback Robertson (26). In this way, after the ball is circulated from the opposite side, a 2-vs-1 numerical superiority is generated out wide against the forward who steps up to defend.

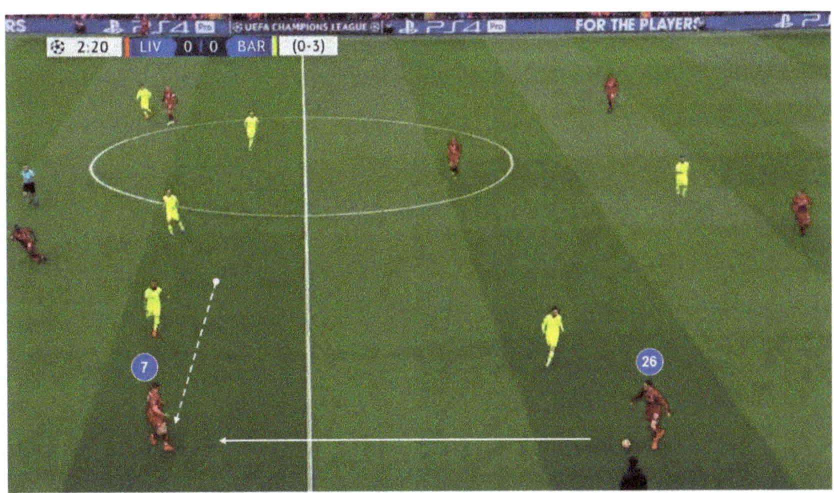

Image 98. Champions League semi-final 2018/19: Liverpool–Barcelona

As we have reviewed with his previous offensive mechanics, Klopp has a penchant for punishing his opponents' outside players. As can be seen in Image 99, when the ball reaches a player out wide, such as the right winger Salah (11) in this example, and the opposing fullback steps up, the attacking midfielder Henderson (14) immediately leaves the interior zone to dismark into the widening interval between the centerback and the fullback. The German coach's Liverpool team uses this movement very frequently to advance in the finishing zone because it's very difficult to defend. In most cases the opposing center midfielder cannot follow him, and the centerback doesn't have time to step up and cover because the center forward is fixing him or because the distance is too far to make this possible.

Image 99. European Super Cup 2019/20: Liverpool–Chelsea

Attacking the space between the centerback and the fullback has yet another variation. As Image 100 shows, when a player on the outside is in possession of the ball, in this case the right back Alexander-Arnold (66), Liverpool looks to provoke the opposing attacking midfielder to step up. The winger on that side, here Salah (11), stays wide to create uncertainty for the outside defender. If he holds his position, it allows the fullback Alexander-Arnold (66) to have an outside-out pass to the foot of the winger Salah (11), who can dribble after receiving the ball to generate advantages. If the opponent's fullback steps up to the winger, a space opens up that can be attacked diagonally, as seen in Image 103, or a player can dismark inside to attract an opponent. In the action shown in Image 100 the center forward Diogo Jota (20), who starts from a position where he is fixing the opposing centerback, dismarks into the interval between the defender and the fullback once all the nearby markers have been dragged away.

Image 100. Champions League group stage 2020/21: Atalanta–Liverpool

Firmino is one of the strikers who has played the most minutes during Klopp's reign at Liverpool. It's no coincidence, since his technical-tactical characteristics offer the German a wide range of possibilities at the strategic level. In addition to being able to threaten in space, his main virtue is his ability to generate synergies with his teammates (wall passes and third-man actions) and to play vertically.

As Image 101 shows, when the opposing midfielders are looking to mark the attacking midfielders, here Milner (7) and Keïta (8), the center forward Firmino (9) drops down and moves into the free space generated between the lines in the central channel. In this way, he ceases to be a player who fixes opponents in the back line and becomes a player who generates numerical superiority with four players in the central channel. If he receives the ball, he is able to quickly take advantage by turning and playing vertically with a pass or a dribble.

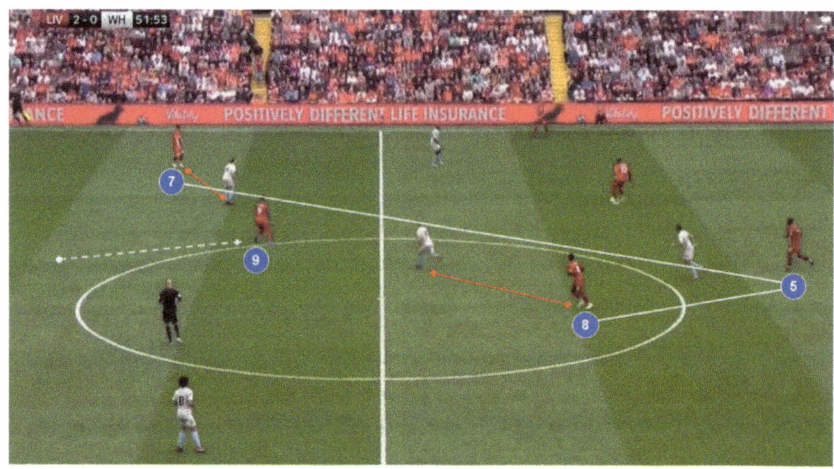

Image 101. Premier League 2018/19: Liverpool–West Ham

Another reason the center forward will stop fixing opponents is to make movements towards the interior channels, with the objective of forming triangles on the sides of the field. As reflected in Image 102, Firmino (9) fulfills this function by checking back to form a triangle out wide with the fullback and the winger on the active side; Robertson (26) and Mané (10), respectively. This action can create a 3-vs-3 or 3-vs-2 situation.

Image 102. Premier League 2017/18: Liverpool–Tottenham

As can be seen in Image 103, when the center forward, in this case Firmino (9), drops down the two wingers get narrower and look to make runs behind their markers towards the central channel, in the intervals between the centerbacks and fullbacks. In this way both outside attackers fix the entire back line in a 2-vs-4 numerical inferiority, which dissuades the defenders from pursuing the center forward.

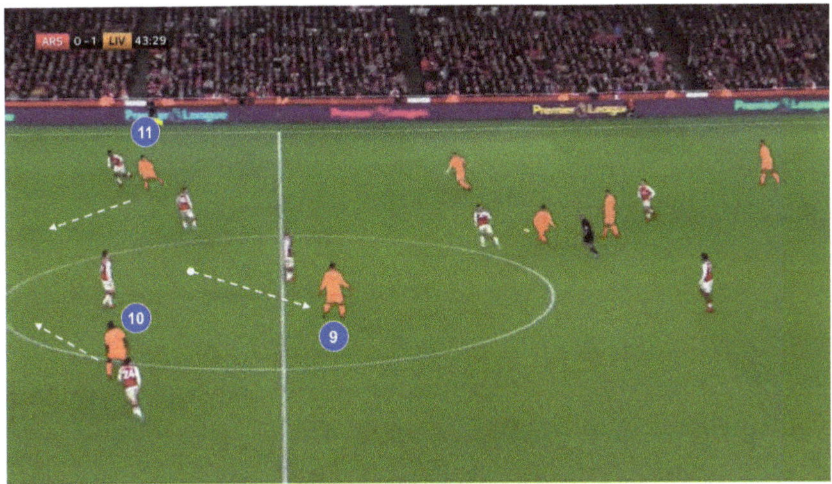

Image 103. Premier League 2017/18: Arsenal–Liverpool

Although Klopp prefers it to be the center forward who drops down, either of the two wingers can also check back to support in the interior channels. An example can be seen in Image 104, as the right winger Salah (11) drops down to generate a numerical superiority with four players.

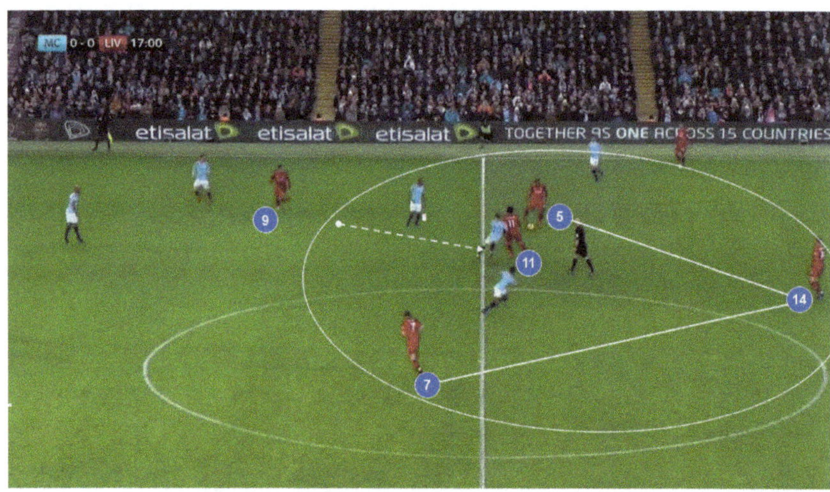

Image 104. Premier League 2018/19: Manchester City–Liverpool

Klopp's game model seeks to be unpredictable at all times. Therefore, his Liverpool alternates progression using vertical combination play with direct play into space. The team generates many scoring chances through long balls from the central defenders towards the zone of offensive advantage (behind the opponent's back line). This is possible thanks to the constant threat that the more distant players (the three attackers) offer the man in possession.

If the ball carrier is a centerback and the wingers are playing wide in the outside channels, the latter will dismark by making outside-in runs into space, generally in front of their markers. Image 105 demonstrates this, as the left centerback Van Dijk (4) exhibits his ability to place the ball into the path of a teammate's run, in this case for the left winger Mané (10).

Image 105. Champions League quarter-final 2018/19: Bayern München–Liverpool

If the center forward doesn't drop down, he can also offer an option for a long pass into space by dismarking through the interval between the centerbacks, as Divock Origi (27) does in Image 106. In this example the left winger Mané (10) makes a similar movement to accompany the Belgian.

Image 106. Premier League 2019/20: Liverpool–Everton

As can be seen in Image 107, if the player in possession is a fullback, in this case Alexander-Arnold (66) on the right, they also have the option of playing directly into space. This variant is usually generated from a combined movement that once again seeks to create uncertainty for the opposing fullback. If the winger on the active side, here Salah (11) on the right, dismarks to support in the outside channel, the attacking midfielder on that side, here Wijnaldum (5), dismarks into the interval between the centerback and the fullback.

Image 107. Champions League semi-final 2017/18: Liverpool–Roma

FINISHING ZONE

In the finishing zone, the main tactical variation stems from the height of the fullbacks. In the final third they move higher, until they've positioned themselves alongside the forward line. In this way the spaces are occupied in a 1-2-3-5 formation. Once Klopp's Liverpool reaches this area, they want to play extremely vertically to generate as many scoring chances as possible. In Klopp's first six years, Liverpool has averaged 16 shots per game (according to whoscored.com).

When facing a low block, the German's squad uses one or two quick actions based on the offensive tactical principles of wall passes, free spaces, and dismarking in behind. In these situations the involvement of the center forward, usually Firmino (9), is essential. As can be seen in Image 108, whoever fulfills this role must have the ability to play with his back to the goal. He must be able to drop back between the lines in the central channel to offer wall passes with the player in possession and to break lines. Generally, these combinations in the central channel are designed so that one of the wingers, in this case Salah (11) on the right, dribbles inside with the ball, overcomes his immediate defender, and creates a clear shooting chance. At the same time, as Image 108 shows, the interior players such as the left attacking midfielder Wijnaldum (5) can also carry out movements to drag their markers and generate free space in the zone where the player with the ball is going.

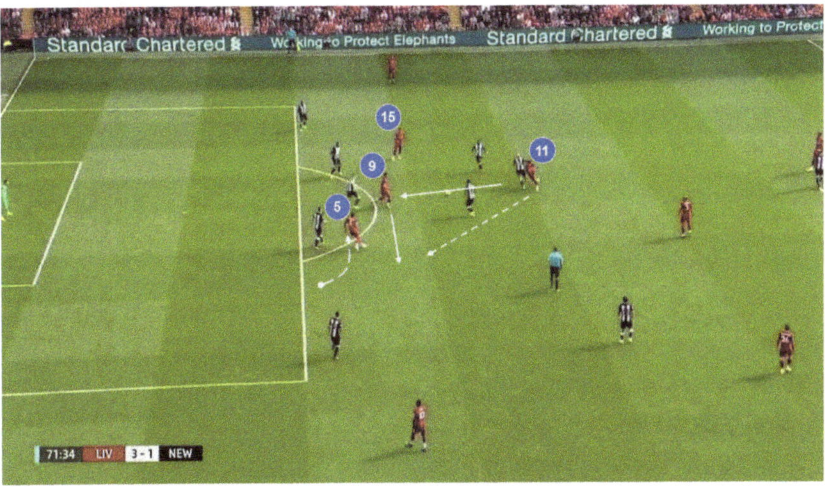

Image 108. Premier League 2019/20: Liverpool–Newcastle

But Klopp's Liverpool prefers to attack on the outside. Throughout the German's first six years at the club the team carried out 72% of their attacks on the flanks (according to whoscored.com). Against defenses playing in a low block, the Reds adhere to the offensive principles of speed of play, width, and depth.

As can be seen in Image 109, the first thing Liverpool looks to do is get behind their opponent's back line, quickly reaching one of the two corners of the field. This can be done with a long ball into space towards a wide player or through dribbling, as the left back Robertson (26) often does. The action shown in Image 109 serves as an example. If the player entering the final third with the ball is able to attack the penalty area from that position, he will do it. If not, he seeks to draw the shifting defense to the strong side.

In Image 109 the German coach wants his team to get the ball to the opposite corner, on the weak side. After having drawn in the opposing defenders, Liverpool passes backwards to initiate a switch of play as quickly as possible. This can be done by circulating the ball outside of the opponent's defensive structure, in which this rule is followed: if you can skip a player, do it. An example is shown in Image 109 as the left centerback, here Van Dijk (4), passes to the right back Alexander-Arnold (66), skipping the other centerback and the defensive midfielder. It's also possible to carry out this switch of play with a direct diagonal ball to the opposite corner.

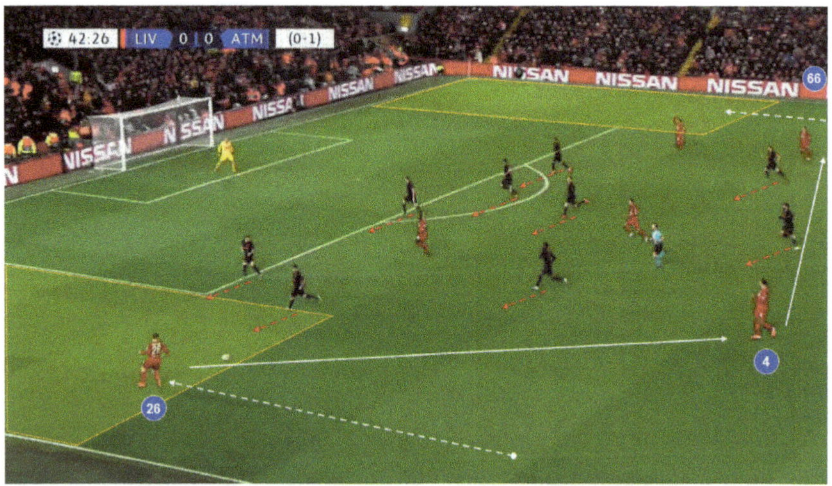

Image 109. Champions League quarter final 2019/20: Liverpool–Atlético de Madrid

With the ball in an outer channel, one of Liverpool's main mechanisms is the formation of offensive triangles to generate situations of numerical superiority (3-vs-2) or equality (3-vs-3). As seen in Image 110, these shapes are generally formed by a player in the outer channel, as the right winger Salah (11) does in this case, and two additional players in the inside channel, here the right back Alexander-Arnold (66), and the right attacking midfielder Oxlade-Chamberlain (15).

Although Klopp's Liverpool can resolve the situation of numerical equality in different ways depending on the specifics of each situation, the most common option is for the player furthest back, here Alexander-Arnold (66), to a pass to the teammate in the outer channel, who in this case is Salah (11). At that moment, it is of vital importance that the most advanced player in the interior channel, here Oxlade-Chamberlain (15), always threatens the space between the opponent's centerback and fullback so that the latter is unsure of whether to step up or not. Depending on the opponent's response, the German's team resolves their situation of superiority in different ways: with the interior player dismarking into space, as Oxlade-Chamberlain (15) does in Image 110; with an outside-in wall pass, as demonstrated in Image 111 between the center forward Firmino (9) and Salah (11), the winger on the active side; or through a 1-vs-1 with the player in the outer channel confronting the fullback, as the right attacking midfielder Henderson (14) does in Image 112.

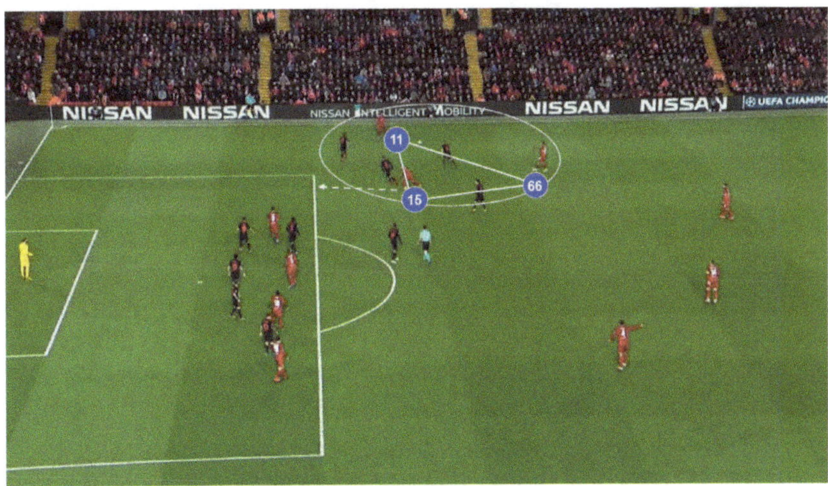

Image 110. Champions League quarter-final 2019/20:
Liverpool–Atlético de Madrid

Image 111. Premier League 2020/21: Chelsea–Liverpool

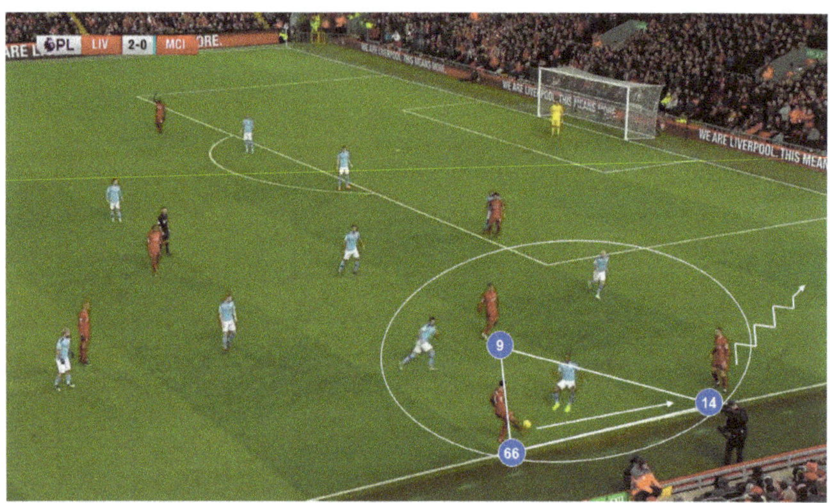

Image 112. Premier League 2019/20: Liverpool–Manchester City

Another possible attacking situation starts when the ball reaches the foot of a winger positioned out wide. Klopp prefers to play with off-footed players on the outside, so they tend to carry the ball inside. Salah and Mané, who have fulfilled these roles most often during the German's cycle at the club, are powerful players who are so intimidating when in possession of the ball in front of goal that they always draw the attention of the nearby defenders. By dribbling inside, a role that can also be carried out by other players, the forwards are guaranteed support in the form of teammates who generate passing lines into space or dismark to create free spaces where the ball carrier can finish with an individual action.

Image 113 reflects this concept. Here the right winger Salah (11) drives inside with the ball at the same time that the attacking midfielder on that side, Milner (7) in this example, dismarks into the interval between the centerback and the fullback. This gives the Egyptian two options: play a pass into the path of that movement or beat the opposing fullback on the strong side and pass to the center forward Xherdan Shaqiri (23).

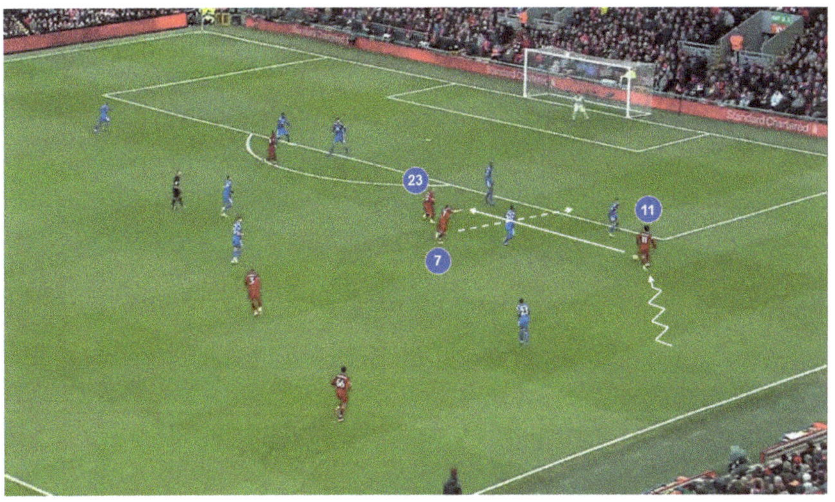

Image 113. Premier League 2018/19: Liverpool–Cardiff

While it is more common for Salah to receive at his feet out wide, Klopp instead prefers that the left winger, a role primarily played by Mané throughout this cycle, receives the ball inside. As can be seen in Image 114, it's very common for whoever fulfills this function, here Mané (10), to occupy the interior zone in front of the penalty area. After receiving the ball, he is able to turn and shoot on goal.

Klopp's Liverpool is in a position to generate this space due to the dismarking movements of the fullback or the attacking midfielders to the outside, which drag the opposing fullback away, and the threat of a ball played in the penalty area, which often deters the centerback on the active side from stepping up.

Image 114. Premier League 2019/20 Southampton–Liverpool

One of the offensive automatisms in the finishing zone that's most representative of Klopp's Liverpool is to constantly dismark into space behind the back line. This is a team that benefits greatly from attacking the zone of offensive advantage.

Dismarking into the interval between the centerback and the fullback on the strong side represents one of the movements most commonly used by the German's team. This is not just a solution when playing within the offensive triangles; it can be used in any situation when facing a low block where the wide player can stretch the distance between those two opponents. As can be seen in Image 115, in these situations the winger on the active side, here Mané (10) on the left, attracts the rival fullback while a player who starts ahead of the ball, in this case the center forward Firmino (9), must attack the free space that is generated.

Image 115. Premier League 2018/19: Fulham–Liverpool

Klopp's teams also execute this dismark into space in the interval between the centerback and the fullback on the weak side. In these maneuvers the distance between the opponents does not increase, since the fullback on the opposite side will always play narrow. For this reason, it's necessary for the player who makes this run to rely on his reaction speed. This is exemplified by the sequence in Image 116 in which the wide player, the right winger Mané (10) in this example, gets a step on his marker and ends up in an advantageous position.

Image 116. Premier League 2018/19: Liverpool–Manchester United

There is also the possibility for the fullback on the active side to attack the zone of offensive advantage by overlapping on the outside. For this to happen, the opponent's fullback needs to be fixed, as can be seen in Image 117: the fullback on the active side, here the right back Alexander-Arnold (66), overlaps to attack the space generated when the right winger Salah (11) fixes the outside defender. The fullback Alexander-Arnold (66) is now ahead of the rest of the players, which means his teammates will not be offside if the ball is passed to the middle. Therefore, the player who receives the ball in this situation usually puts in a low cross between the goalkeeper and the back line towards a striker with a positional advantage. In this example, the Englishman crosses to the center forward Firmino (9), who gets in behind the fullback on the weak side.

Image 117. Champions League quarter-final 2018/19:
Liverpool–Oporto

The second mechanism identified with Klopp's Liverpool consists of crosses from the fullbacks. As we have seen, the initial objective of the German's team is to reach the corners of the field. From that position, the high technical quality of the fullbacks makes them the principal crossers of the ball. Although they can deliver the ball to any of the three shooting zones, the preference is for the fullbacks to deliver the ball to the far post (with right footed players crossing from the right and left footed players crossing from the left), as the left fullback Robertson (26) can be seen doing in Image 118.

Ideally, the cross should be sent from a point in front of the line of attackers because this allows them to score more easily. Since the trajectory of the ball comes from ahead of the players as they charge the penalty area, they can finish while facing the goal.

Image 118. Premier League 2019/20: Manchester United–
Liverpool

An alternative to the conventional cross from a fullback used by
Klopp's Liverpool is to send the ball beyond the opposition's back
line for a player advancing from the second line of attackers. As
can be seen in Image 119, the player in possession, here the right
back Alexander-Arnold (66), sends in a low cross for the advancing
midfield player, the left attacking midfielder Wijnaldum (5).

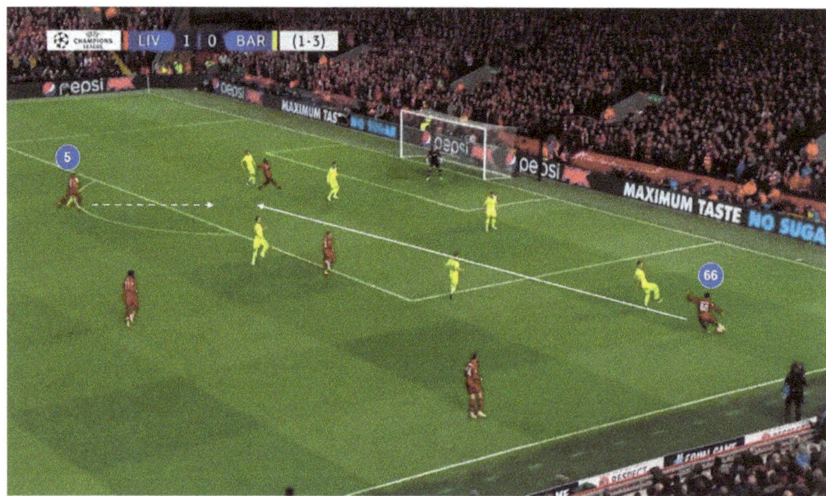

Image 119. Champions League semi-final 2018/19: Liverpool–
Barcelona

When sending players into the penalty area, Klopp maintains the same four-player (3 + 1) structure that he used at Borussia Dortmund. The ideal situation is for the three strikers to charge the penalty area in a line, accompanied by an attacking midfielder from the second line, although there can be constant interchanges of position. As Image 120 shows, the three attackers seek numerical equality and occupy the three shooting zones. The winger on the strong side usually attacks the near post, with the center forward near the penalty spot and the weak side winger at the far post.

Image 120. Champions League final 2017/18: Real Madrid–Liverpool

In situations of numerical inferiority inside the penalty area, Klopp's players have two ways of obtaining a positional advantage. First, they seek to gain position on the first defender or whoever covers the near post when they attack the intervals. As can be seen in Image 121, in a situation of 2-vs-3 numerical inferiority in which the winger from the strong side, in this case the right winger Salah (11), is outside the penalty area, the center forward Firmino (9) makes a movement to finish in front of his defender at the near post.

Image 121. Champions League quarter-final 2018/19: Oporto–Liverpool

The second option is to get in behind the last defender. Image 122 exemplifies this, in another situation of 2-vs-3 numerical inferiority: the winger on the weak side, here Salah (11) on the right, dismarks to the far post behind his marker.

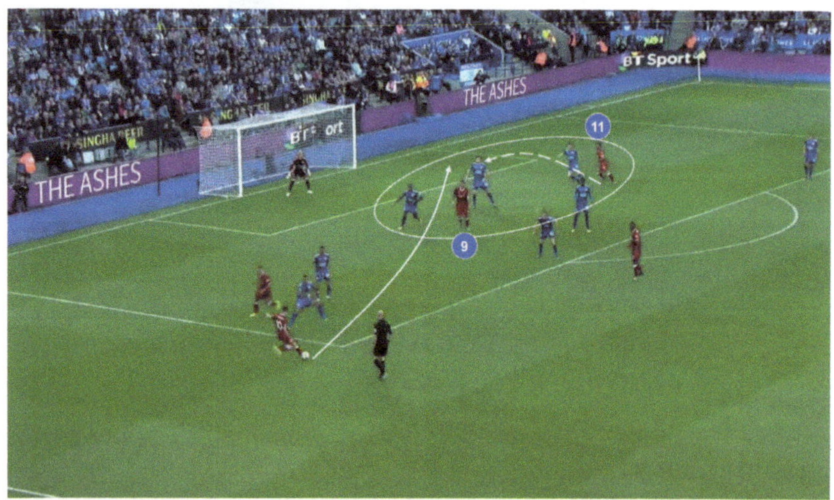

Image 122. Premier League 2017/18: Leicester–Liverpool

When the team is about to execute a cross from out wide, the weak side fullback narrows his position towards the front of the penalty area, as the left back Robertson (26) can be seen doing in Image 123. Because the majority of crosses go to the far post, these players are in an advantageous position to regain possession and send the ball back into the area in the event that the cross does not generate a shot or the goalkeeper deflects the ball to the sides. In this way, there may be two or even three crosses in one sequence. By crossing the ball multiple times, the team can take advantage of defensive disorganization and unmarked players, since it switches the focus of attention from one side to the other. If the ball is cleared towards the middle, it's common to finish the play with a shot on goal.

Image 123. Champions League quarter-final 2019/20:
Liverpool–Atlético de Madrid

However, one of the most unique automatisms of Klopp's Liverpool is when the weak side fullback charges into the area to get on the end of a cross at the far post. As can be seen in Image 124, it's common for the left back Robertson (26) to dismark into this area when a "closed" cross (a left-footed player crossing from the right side) is anticipated.

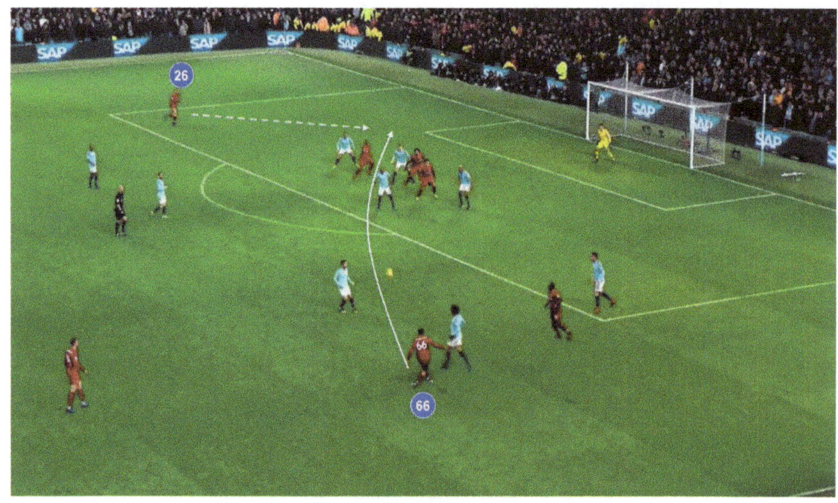

Image 124. Premier League 2018/19: Manchester City–Liverpool

Offensive transition

The offensive transition has a decisive influence on the game model of Klopp's teams. But due to their elevated percentage of possession, counter-attacking is not a priority at Liverpool: it is used when needed. His teams in Germany and in England both shared the same style and basic principles, although with the Reds the German coach has developed certain nuances that have evolved this phase towards higher levels of effectiveness and efficiency.

For Klopp, these actions always start with the principle of applying the same system used in the defensive phase to the transition phase. At Borussia Dortmund he used the 1-4-4-2 due to its compatibility with a counterattack employing four players. In contrast, his Liverpool counters with three players from a 1-4-5-1.

This decision has allowed the German to add a midfielder to the defensive phase without altering his principle of launching offensive transitions through three channels. In this way, this adjustment has not interfered with the sub-principles of where to counterattack according to the channel where the ball is won: if it happens inside, Liverpool tries to finish on the outside; if it happens outside, they try to finish on the inside or on the opposite side. With three attackers, the proper spatial distribution is respected in order to move the ball from one side to the other, passing through the central channel or arriving directly after a diagonal ball played between the interior channels.

Although Klopp's Liverpool often presses high, the ball is usually recovered in situations where they are defending in a medium or low block. As was the case at Borussia Dortmund, Klopp attaches great importance to the first pass after winning the ball. If possible, that first pass should be sent forward. If this is not possible, there needs to be a touch to get the ball out of the recovery zone and then play vertically.

The big difference between Klopp's counterattacks at Borussia Dortmund and those at Liverpool lie in the number of passes made by each team. The Reds take fewer touches and develop fewer situations with a distant third man in support, instead favoring greater verticality by playing balls into space, dismarking between the intervals, and dribbling at the back line.

The characteristics of the attackers that Klopp has at Liverpool also make this change possible. Both Mané and Salah, who have most often fulfilled the winger function throughout the cycle, are players who are self-sufficient with the ball and are capable of counterattacking in situations of numerical inferiority.

If Liverpool manages to steal the ball from the back line as a result of pressing in a high block, they look to finish quickly. If the ball recovery occurs in the central channel, the play typically ends with a pass and a shot or with an individual action by the player

who won the ball. In Image 125 we can see how the winger on the active side, who in this case is Mané (10), manages to steal a bad back pass from the opposing midfielder and finishes the play with two touches.

On the other hand, if the ball is won in an outside channel, Klopp's team also looks to finish inside by dribbling or passing into the central channel.

Image 125. Premier League 2017/18: Liverpool–Manchester City

In both the low and medium blocks, if opponents are in the recovery zone where the ball is stolen, the first objective is to pass the ball out of that zone. This is usually done with a vertical delivery to the center forward in the central channel, which is one of the counterattack variants.

In the action shown in Image 126, the center forward Firmino (9) drops down to open a passing line with the player in possession after the ball leaves the recovery zone. In these situations, the decisions and actions of this player depend on the space and time available: if he is not pressured, he can turn and send a pass into space in the outside channels where the wingers are positioned, as with this pass to the left winger Mané (10); if he is marked, he can act as the third man to play the ball to another teammate who is facing forward and can send the ball deep to the outside attackers.

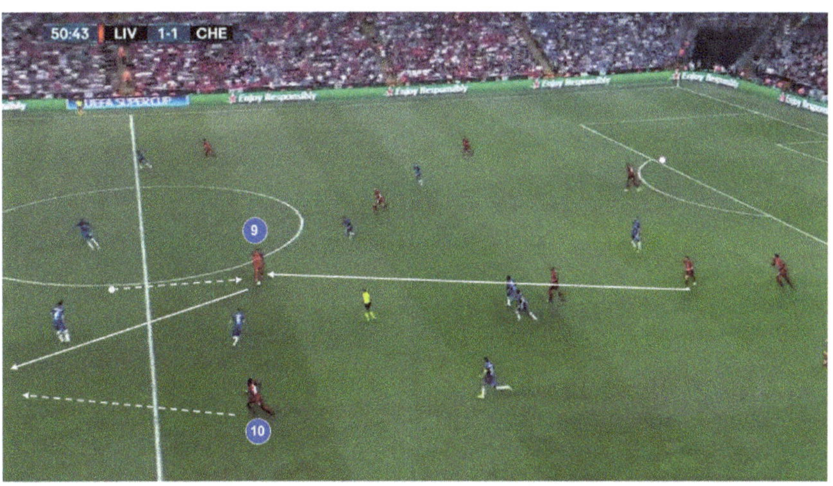

Image 126. European Supercup 2019/20: Liverpool–Chelsea

If the player who recovers the ball is not pressured he can progresses directly with the ball, without the need for any of the three attackers to drop down. When the ball is stolen in the outside channels, it's very common to play a deep outside-out pass to the winger on the active side through the interval between the opponent's centerback and fullback. This is exemplified by the sequence in Image 127 between the right fullback Alexander-Arnold (66) and the right winger Salah (11).

Image 127. Premier League 2020/21: Manchester United–
Liverpool

In the playing model of Klopp's Liverpool, the ideal counterattack involves three players. As can be seen in Image 128, the distribution of players is as follows: the center forward, here Firmino (9), occupies the central channel, with the left winger Mané (10) and the right winger Salah (11) are each positioned within different interior channels.

The alternative to counterattacking with a ball played into space is to run with the ball. In those situations, as shown in Image 128, Klopp prioritizes carrying the ball through the central channel, since this always gives the player in possession two passing options. The movements of the wingers are always from the outside-in.

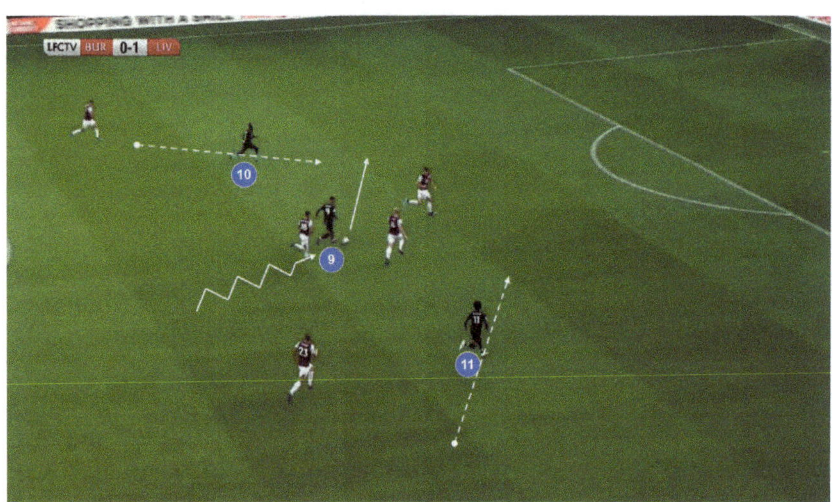

Image 128. Premier League 2019/20: Burnley–Liverpool

If more than three players are involved in the execution of the counterattack, as can be seen in Image 129, Klopp's Liverpool tries to maintain their rules about carrying the ball through the center and maintaining spatial distribution in all three channels. In this example the movements of the left winger Mané (19) and the right winger Salah (11) will also be from the outside-in. For his part, the center forward Firmino (9) will usually dismark between the centerbacks, from the inside out.

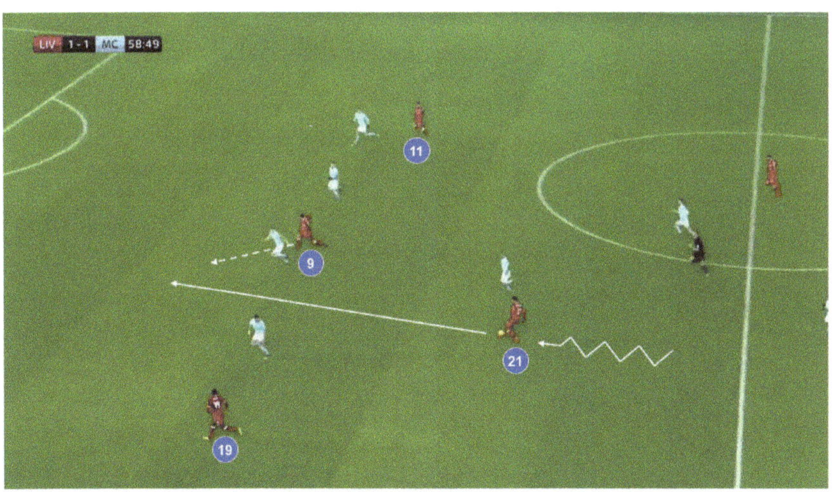

Image 129. Premier League 2017/18: Liverpool–Manchester City

As can be seen in Image 130, if it's a winger running with the ball through an outside channel, as Mané (10) does on the left, the pass will be played inside for the center forward, in this case Origi (27), who is dismarking in the interval between the centerbacks.

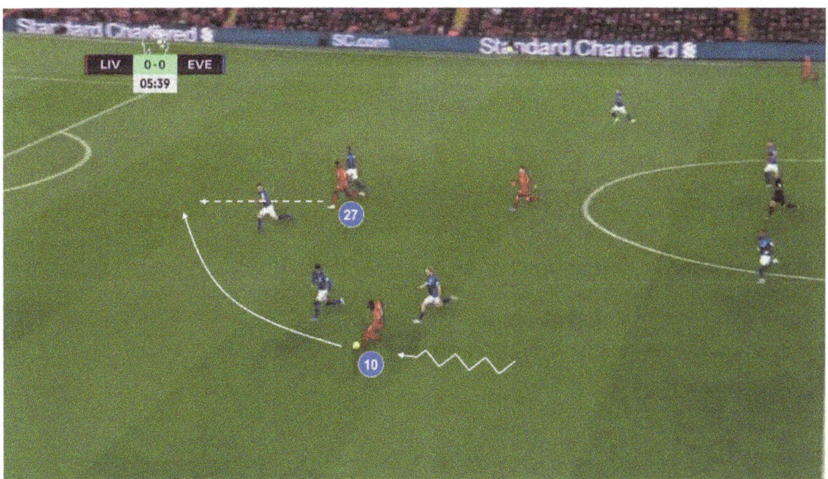

Image 130. Premier League 2019/20: Liverpool–Everton

On many occasions when possession is won out wide, the ball will exit the recovery zone through a pass to the fullback on the opposite side. These players are also frequently deployed in the counterattack. As can be seen in Image 131, the fullbacks, like Alexander-Arnold (66) here on the right, will often carry the ball through an outside channel. This mainly occurs in situations where the center forward drops down and there are only two players in front of the ball. Since it's not possible to occupy all three channels, both wingers get narrow to prioritize attacking the central channel.

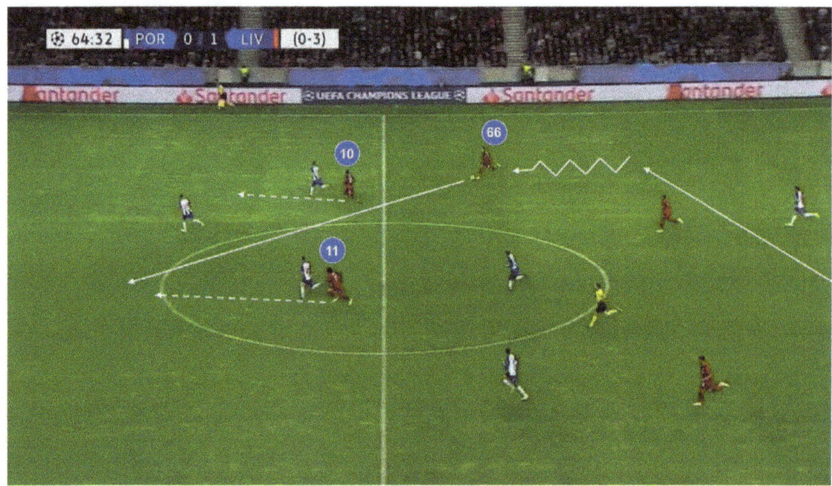

Image 131. Champions League quarter-final 2018/19: Oporto–Liverpool

Klopp's Liverpool has a characteristic feature when counterattacking from an opponent's corner kick. As can be seen in Image 132, they defend corners with the whole team, placing eight players in the penalty area and keeping the two wingers higher up, with one covering the top of the area at the near post, as the left winger Mané (10) does, and the other covering the top of the area at the far post, as the right winger Salah (11) does. All players are part of the defensive block.

In this way, the German's team invites the opponent to place fewer players in defensive positions downfield. Usually, opponents will leave either two defenders back, staggered vertically, or just a single player. This decision creates a huge amount of space for Liverpool to counterattack from their low block. When there's a clearance or a rebound, both wingers remain poised to gain possession and counterattack with both a lot of open field and in situations of numerical equality (2-vs-2) or superiority (2-vs-1).

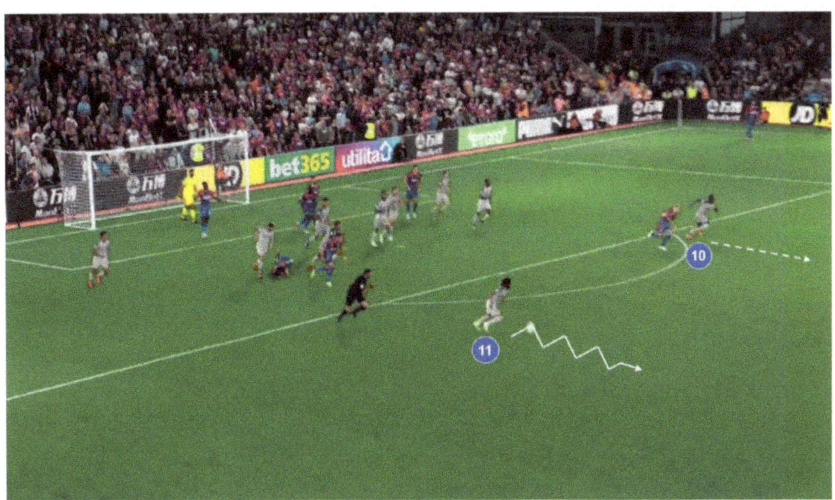

Image 132. Premier League 2018/19: Crystal Palace–Liverpool

As can be seen in Image 133, in 2-vs-2 or 3-vs-2 situations the attacker in the central channel, who in this example is the right winger Salah (11), will cross in front of the player with the ball, here the left winger Oxlade-Chamberlain (15), to drag a marker away and open up space for an individual action or a pass to the free man. If the opponent does not follow this run into space, there is also the possibility for this player to receive a through-ball.

Image 133. Premier League 2017/18: Leicester–Liverpool

As shown in Image 134, the solution for situations of 2-vs-1 superiority is for the player running with the ball, as the left winger Mané (19) does in this example, to fix the opposing defender until reaching the edge of the penalty area and then lay the ball off. This behavior by the player on the ball is key, so that the opponent does not have time to recover their position after the pass is made. The other player accompanying the attack, here the right winger Salah (11), must not stray offside.

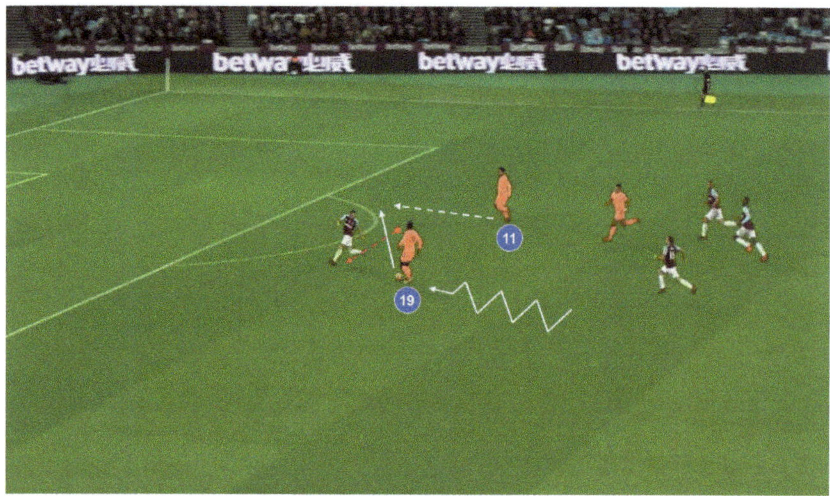

Image 134. Premier League 2017/18: West Ham–Liverpool

Defensive phase

Systems

The defensive phase of Klopp's Liverpool is characterized by its dual functionality and, above all, by its solidity. Before the German coach's arrival, the Reds possessed a powerful attack but a deficient and limited defense. In the two seasons before his arrival and at the beginning of his cycle, the team from the northwest of England conceded 50, 48 and 50 goals respectively (according to whoscored.com).

Through tactical training, Klopp's initial task was to create a defensive structure capable of conceding fewer goals. Starting with the subsequent campaign, Liverpool began to reduce the number of goals conceded. For example: in 2016/17 they conceded 42; in 2017/18, 38; in 2018/19, 22, and in 2019/20, the year they won the Premier League, 33 (whoscored.com). As their dominance has grown, the team has surrendered fewer and fewer goals.

Klopp's Liverpool has become such a complete team that they can defend at any height; in a high, medium, or low block, and are capable of adapting these blocks to different situations within the same match. For the German coach, defending well doesn't just mean giving up fewer goals, but also "making opponents weaker" (quoted by Neveling, 2016). This offensive interpretation signifies developing the defensive phase with an eye towards counterattacking. Through pressure in a high or medium block, Klopp's Liverpool is able to take the initiative in matches and dominate their opponents, generating useful contexts for their offensive transitions.

In his first season in England, 2015/16, Klopp continued to frequently use the same 1-4-1-3-2 system from his final stage at Borussia Dortmund (Image 48). However, his most commonly used system for pressing in a high block at Liverpool is now the 1-4-3-3 with players in intermediate zones. This consists of placing the attackers within the intervals between two or more defenders and carrying out pressing movements based on the movement of the ball. In this way, and as Guardiola explains, the players of the team in possession appear to be open until the moment they are pressed. They do not have a clear reference of who their defender is. Additionally, the players from the team in the defensive phase also have the possibility of challenging two or more players at a time.

As can be seen in Image 135, the 1-4-3-3 system allows the configuration of inverted triangles in 2 + 1 microstructures, initially protecting the central and interior channels. With three players in the first line of pressure, it's not possible to maintain short distances to each other, so inside passes can be played in the intervals between the forwards; here Mané (10), Firmino (9), and Salah (11) as the left winger, center forward and right winger, respectively. Faced with this reality, Klopp looks to compensate with his attacking midfielders: in this example Wijnaldum (5) on the left and Henderson (14) on the right step up to pressure if the line of forwards is overcome. The defensive midfielder, Fabinho (3) in this action, does the same if either of the two attacking midfielders is overcome in the central channel.

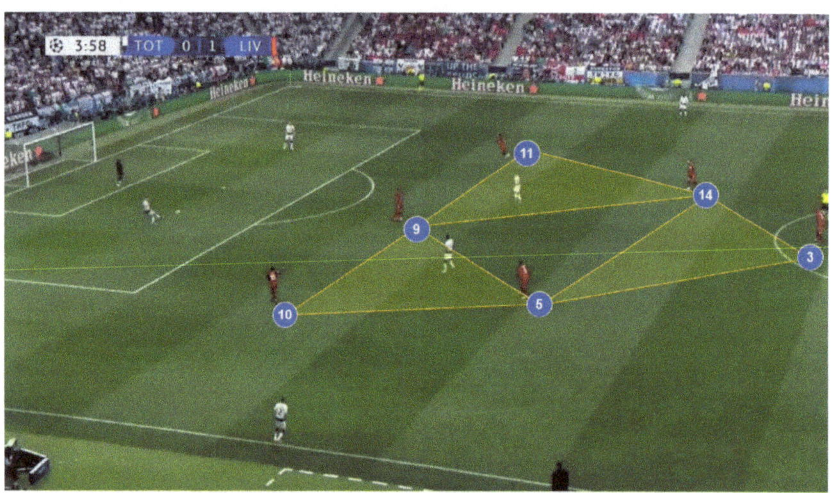

Image 135. Champions League final 2018/19: Tottenham—Liverpool

When defending in a medium block, Klopp has indeed varied his systems depending on the characteristics of each opponent. To ensure he can counterattack with three attackers and to make it easier for players to shift from one formation to another, in the defensive phase he has always used systems that are compatible with the 1-4-3-3. Generally, his Liverpool have defended in a 1-4-5-1 formation, with both wingers simply dropping down. As each season has gone by, their ability to counterattack has become an asset of enormous importance. For this reason both wingers, though especially the right winger (usually Salah), have moved to position themselves slightly forward in a staggered 1-4-3-3, rather than remaining in line with the three midfielders.

Against opponents with players who occupy the space between the lines well, Klopp can use a 1-4-1-4-1 variation, dropping back his defensive midfielder to mark zonally or to apply pressure in that intermediate space.

In recent seasons the arrival of different strikers, notably Diogo Jota and Luis Díaz, has given Klopp the option of playing with four forwards. In these situations the German usually uses the 1-4-4-2 system to accommodate the four attackers and maintain as balanced a structure as possible in the defensive phase.

When defending in a low block, Klopp's Liverpool prioritizes the 1-4-5-1 system, with all the lines close together. There is no need to leave a striker detached from the defensive block, as both wingers are primed for deployment in the event of a counterattack.

Organized defense

HIGH BLOCK

The most substantial difference between Klopp's Borussia Dortmund and Liverpool is in the height at which they begin to be proactive. While at Borussia Dortmund the preference was to recover the ball in a medium block, at Liverpool the intention is to recover the ball up high; the closer to the opponent's goal, the better! The situations in which the Reds apply high pressure are: when the opponent wants to start their buildout from a goal kick; when they force their opponent to pass back from a medium block position; in contexts where the opponent is emotionally weak; or when faced with the need to overcome an adverse result.

According to Pepijn Lijnders (2022), the key to the success of this very aggressive and courageous form of pressing depends on the last two meters of pressure. What they call "massive pressure" needs to happen. That is to say: make the effort to close down the opponent in those last two meters "at maximum speed and with the greatest desire to win the ball." Hence one

of the main reasons for Klopp's preference for energetic players, especially in midfield.

As explained by Lijnders (2022), in Klopp's Liverpool game model the team is divided into two blocks in order to carry out high pressing: one block is made up of seven players, with a line of four defenders and a line of three midfielders; the other is made up of the line of three forwards. Klopp requires his three attackers to defend 5 or 6 opponents.

As can be seen in Image 136, the forwards start in a situation of numerical inferiority when pressing high in a 1-4-3-3 formation. The way to resolve this disadvantage is by positioning the players in intermediate areas, as we have already seen. The initiative to start the press in a high block falls to the winger on the side where the opponent is building out.

Image 136 reflects the starting positions for the members of the first line of pressure. The wingers, here Mané (10) on the left and Salah (11) on the right, are each situated in an interval between a centerback and a fullback. In this case it's the Egyptian who initiates the press with a run to pressure the defender, closing the passing line to the fullback on the outside. The intention of Klopp's Liverpool is always to funnel the buildout to the inside, where they have more players and a greater chance of winning the ball. Additionally, the center forward, in this case Firmino (9), does not step up on the wide centerbacks. Instead he maintains a position that focuses on the penalty area, marking the opposing defensive midfielder and preventing the opponent from using this player to build out through the middle.

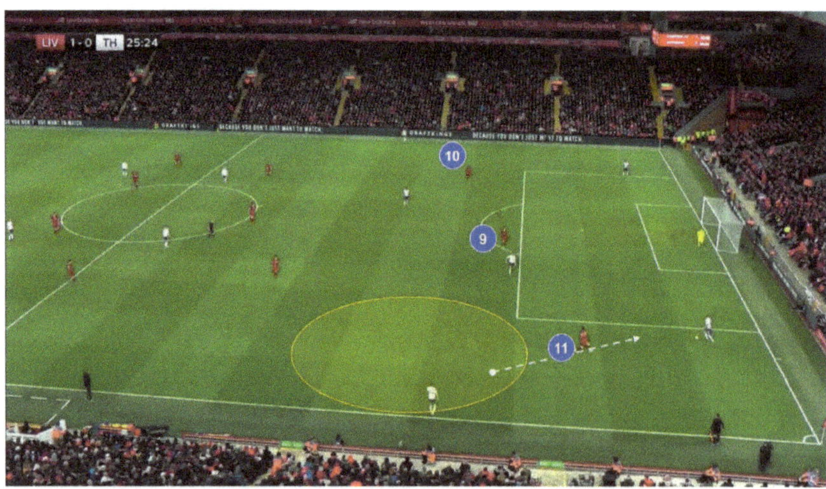

Image 136. Premier League 2017/18: Liverpool–Tottenham

However, the movement of the winger on the active side, Salah (11) in the previous example, to step up to the centerback generates a spatial imbalance in the outside channel, leaving the opposing fullback in that area as the free man. Most teams try to skip Liverpool's pressure by finding that fullback with an inside-out third-man action (through one of the central midfielders checking back to the ball). Thanks to their triangular 2 + 1 microstructures, the Reds are able to successfully defend those situations in different ways.

As can be seen in Image 137, if the opposing fullback drops down in anticipation of the centerback passing inside, the winger on the active side, here Mané (10) on the left, simultaneously drops down to prevent the third man action with the fullback as the attacking midfielder in that zone, in this case Milner (7), steps up to pressure the ball. As a consequence, Liverpool prevents progression, forces a back pass, and then reverts to their initial 1-4-3-3 setup with players in intermediate areas.

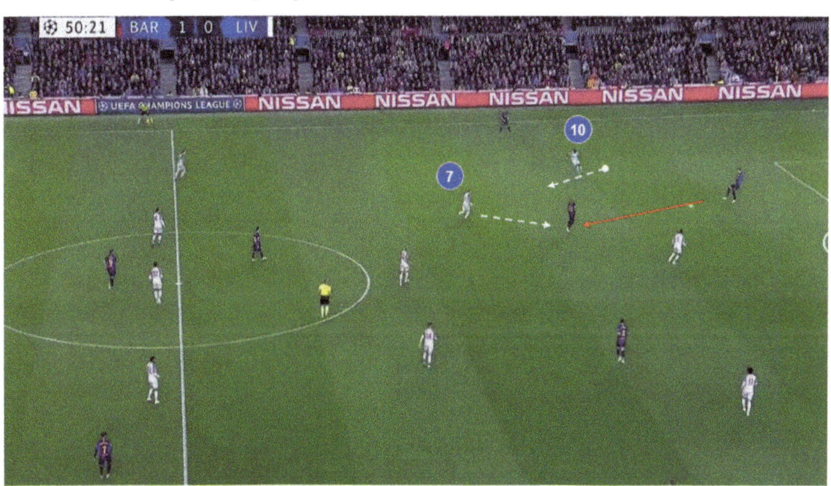

Image 137. Champions League semi-final 2018/19: Barcelona– Liverpool

As can be seen in Image 138, the players from the second line, as in this example with the attacking midfielder Keïta (8), try to bend their runs to the outside of the opponent as they press, in anticipation of the third-man layoff to the fullback. If the player from the front line who has been overcome, here the left winger Mané (10), is not far away from the opponent in possession, he can defend from in front of the ball, dropping down to create a 2-vs-1.

Image 138. Premier League 2020/21: Liverpool–Leeds

As can be seen in Image 139, if the opposing fullback drops down but is at a distance where the winger who's been overcome by the ball cannot regain his defensive position, the attacking midfielder on that side, here Milner (7) who is pressing the opponent who drops down to support, will adjust his run to the outside. In these situations the winger and the attacking midfielder exchange positions until they have an opportunity to reorganize.

Image 139. Premier League 2018/19: Liverpool–Manchester City

As can be seen in Image 140, if the fullback on the strong side, in this case Alexander-Arnold (66), is not fixed by the winger then he can also pressure the opposing fullback in the same situation when there is an inside-outside third man action. The Liverpool player who fulfills this function only adopts this position when he has a high probability of intercepting the pass or when the opponent has his back turned, with a poor body profile.

This way of defending third-man actions is the least common and the most risky because when the fullback steps up, the team loses a member of the back line at a time when they are situated very high up the field, assuming the risk of being exposed to a 3-vs-3 or 3-vs-2 situation with plenty of space behind them. Even so, the players on the back line, both the centerbacks and fullbacks, will follow their marks out of their zone if they drop down to support.

Until the 2018/19 season the defensive midfielder used to be the player who stepped up on the opponent's pivot, as exemplified in Image 140 with Henderson (14). For their part, the attacking midfielders would generally mark more zonally against their counterparts from the rival team.

Image 140. Champions League qualifying round 2017/18: Liverpool–Hoffenheim

As can be seen in Image 141, when faced with a switch of play that starts with a back pass from the opposing fullback to the centerback, the center forward, in this case Mané (10), steps up to the nearest centerback. Meanwhile the winger on the weak side, here Oxlade-Chamberlain (15) on the left, follows the other centerback and will even pressure the goalkeeper if necessary, closing the passing line to the outside. The second line also moves forward to close down space and pressure the opponents who drop down to support.

Image 141. European Supercup 2019/20: Liverpool–Chelsea

As explained previously, the greatest vulnerability in Klopp's preferred 1-4-3-3 pressing system is in the outside channels. Another of the mechanisms that the opponents use is to push their fullbacks up high to increase the distances between themselves and the centerbacks. As can be seen in Image 142, Liverpool encourages the opponents to start the buildout with a long switch of play to one side, since this is a fairly risky pass. Generally the player who pressures ball is the attacking midfielder on that side, Wijnaldum (5) in this action. As the ball travels, this midfielder has enough time to get there while the wide player in that zone, here the left winger Mané (10), can also drop back to create a 2-vs-1 situation that is very complicated for the opposing fullback to resolve.

Image 142. European Super Cup 2019/20: Liverpool–Chelsea

As a general rule, the center forward does not usually step up to pressure the rival centerbacks. Instead, his function is to mark the defensive midfielder. If he decides to press a centerback, it generates free space for the rival pivot and provides a potential escape route for the opponent. To compensate for this situation, when the center forward, here Firmino (9), releases his mark then a player from the second line, in this case the defensive midfielder Can (23), automatically moves up to prevent the opponent from turning and progressing, as seen in Image 143.

Image 143. Premier League 2017/18: Liverpool–Manchester City

Against opponents who play with three centerbacks, Liverpool adjusts their high press in a very similar way. As Image 144 shows, the center forward, in this case Firmino (9), keeps the passing line to the opponent's defensive midfielder closed. Instead of occupying the interval between a centerback and a fullback, the wingers, as reflected by Salah (11) on the right, will position themselves between two defenders and press the central player with a bent run that allows them to cover the passing line to the outer member of the back line. The fullbacks match up with the wingbacks, while the players in the second line remain in intermediate positions on the inside.

Image 144. Champions League quarter-final 2020/21: Leipzig–Liverpool

MEDIUM BLOCK

Klopp's Liverpool frequently defends in a medium block. Although they will initially attempt to press in a high block, if the opponent manages to play out, Klopp's team falls back as quickly as possible into a medium block behind the ball. The Reds are physically and mentally prepared to put in the effort required to press in a high block, but it's impossible to maintain that approach for an entire match, so they also alternate the high press with a medium block setup.

For Klopp's Liverpool, ceding the opponent's starting zone has certain advantages. In particular, by enticing the opponent to move forward they increase the space available in the zone of offensive advantage if they can win the ball. In a medium block, the German coach's plan is for the first line of pressure to provoke the mistake and for the second or third line to win the ball.

Generally, their defensive attitude in a medium block is passive and the main objective is to prevent the opponent from progressing. When the ball is outside the defensive structure, Liverpool allows it to circulate and directs the opponent towards the outer channels. In this situation they maintain a zonal defense based on shifting, covering passing lines, and inviting the opponent to make mistakes by playing very difficult vertical passes. Faced with the threat of an opponent playing through the middle, the second line adopts a mixed approach and players are allowed to step up from their zone. When the opponents move out wide, the intention of Klopp's players is to avoid being overtaken by both the ball and their marks.

As can be seen in Image 145, the medium block usually organizes itself in an area of approximately 40x25 meters. In this way the players can stay narrow and close, accumulating teammates on the strong side to prevent progression while leaving the weak side free. Barring situations of a back-pass from the opponent's winger to the centerback or poor positioning from the defenders, Liverpool have no intention of stealing the ball by pressing the defensive line when defending in a medium block.

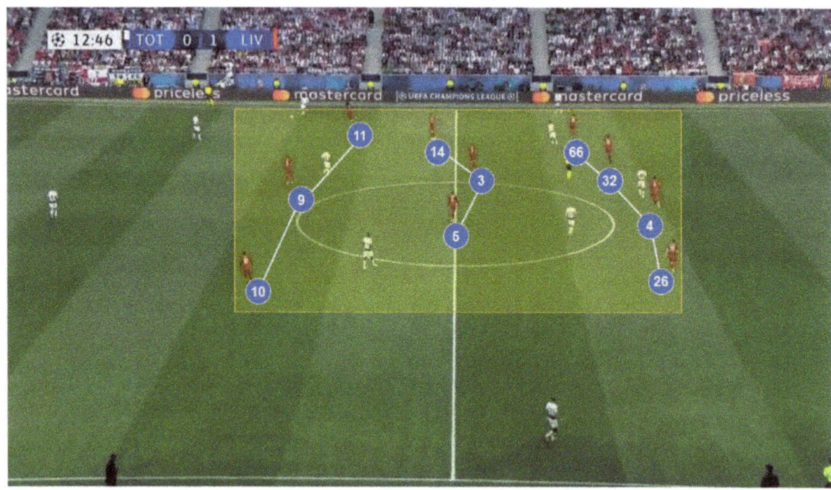

Image 145. Champions League final 2018/19: Tottenham–
Liverpool

When the medium block is situated in the opponent's half of the field in a 1-4-3-3, the wingers stay in advanced positions within the intervals between the centerbacks and fullbacks. With that positioning, Klopp's players seek to cover the direct passing lines to the outer channel when the opponent keeps their fullbacks high or has two players on the outside.

This is reflected in the action in Image 146, in which the opponent's left centerback Sergio Ramos (4) has two options to pass: to the left back Marcelo (12) who is positioned high up the field, or back to the left attacking midfielder Tony Kroos (8). Liverpool's right winger Salah (11) prioritizes covering the most vertical passing line towards Marcelo (12), as this pass would allow the ball to overtake him. On the other hand, if the ball goes to Kroos (8), the Egyptian will have time to pressure the German and his own fullback can step up on the Brazilian. In the event that an opponent appears behind Salah (11) as the third man to play an inside-out pass, Klopp's team can apply any of the strategies for defending the third man that we have previously reviewed.

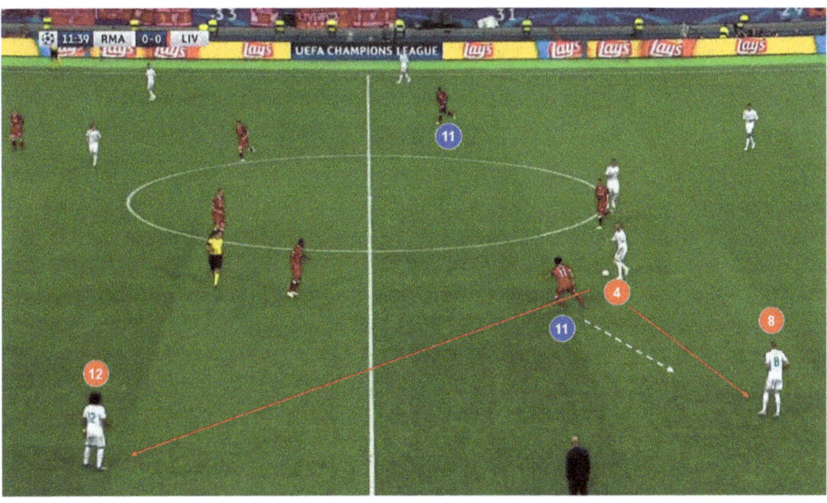

Image 146. Champions League final 2017/18: Real Madrid–
Liverpool

When the medium block organizes more in its own half of the field the wingers, here Mané (10) on the left and Salah (11) on the right, drop down to form a 1-4 -5-1, as can be seen in Image 147. When the ball overcomes the center forward Firmino (9), then the player in the same channel as the ball, in this case the defensive midfielder Fabinho (3), steps up to press the opponent in possession. The two nearby teammates then attempt to narrow the interval to negate the free space that this generates. If the ball travels to another channel then Fabinho (3), the player who has stepped up, will return to his position while someone in the new channel steps up, a maneuver carried out here by the left attacking midfielder Wijnaldum (5).

If the opponent passes backwards, the pressing player can step up again on the centerback, covering the passing line and thus allowing his own defensive lines to advance. If the opponent manages to thread the ball into the space that opens behind the player who steps up, the closest free teammate in the back line (a centerback or a fullback) takes a step forward.

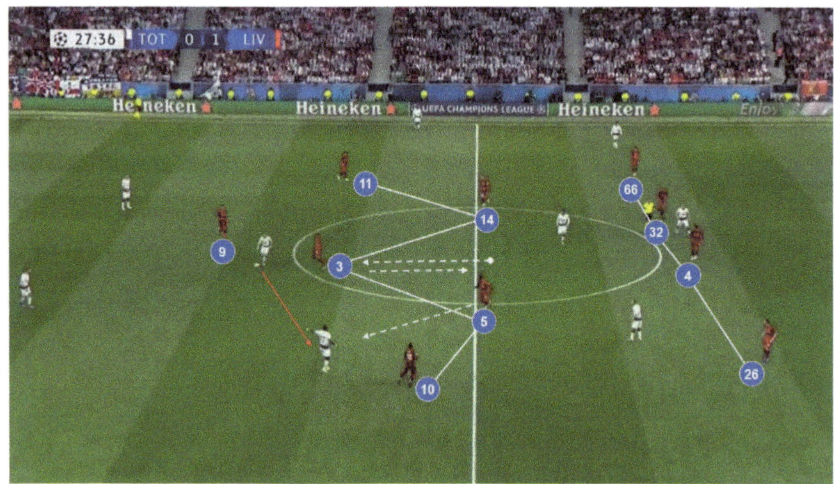

Image 147. Champions League final 2018/19: Tottenham–
Liverpool

When Klopp opts to defend with a medium block in a 1-4-4-2, the principles are the same but with variations in how the players shift. As can be seen in Image 148, the two attackers in the front line, here the center forward Salah (11) and the attacking midfielder Firmino (9), perform alternating "V" shaped movements to direct the ball towards the wings. The objective is to prevent the opponent's progression, since the opposing defensive midfielder is always marked, and to improve the opportunities to steal the ball when the opposing fullbacks have it.

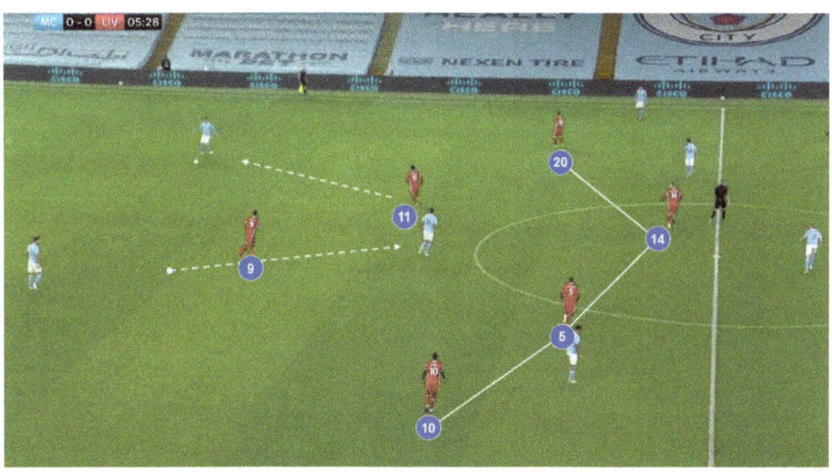

Image 148. Premier League 2020/21: Manchester City–Liverpool

If an opponent progresses down the central channel while dribbling past the first line of pressure, the block falls back until the center midfielder in the same channel as the ball steps up on the opposition. This can be seen in Image 149, in an action where the defensive midfielder Henderson (14) pushes up and the two attacking midfielders, Milner (7) on the left and Oxlade-Chamberlain (21) on the right, move inside to balance the line.

Image 149. Champions League quarter-final 2017/18: Liverpool–Manchester City

Positional exchanges represent another common defensive principle for Klopp's Liverpool. Although the German coach starts with a zonal defense, he places more importance on the rational and balanced occupation of space on the strong side. As we have already seen, the wingers stay high in many situations when in a medium block. This occurs more frequently on the right side with Salah (11), which opens up a lot of space in the outer channel. As can be seen in Image 150, if the fullback on the active side, here Alexander-Arnold (66) on the right, moves up in the outside channel, a series of linked defensive exchanges take place. The nearest central defender, in this case the right centerback Lovren (6), moves up to press the opponent attacking the free space behind the fullback, while the defensive midfielder Henderson (14) takes this defender's place. In this way, they attempt to prevent the opponent's progression so that the players who have been overcome can recover.

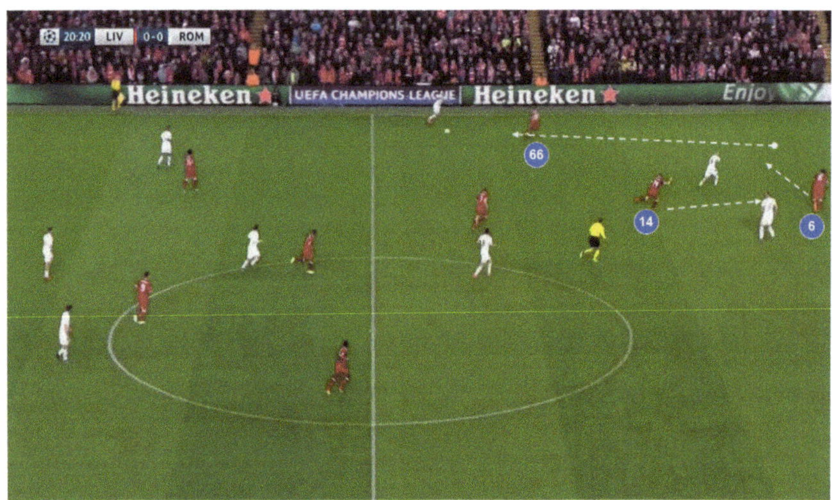

Image 150. Champions League semi-final 2017/18: Liverpool–Roma

As can be seen in Image 151, in situations where the medium block is organized in a 1-4-1-4-1 system, the positional exchange usually only involves a movement by the defensive midfielder, here Henderson (14). This player will follow an opponent between the lines who tries to attack the interval between a center back and fullback.

Image 151. Premier League 2016/17: Liverpool–Manchester City

As shown in Image 152, the vulnerabilities in the 1-4-5-1 formation are: the spaces to the sides of the center forward; the two zones between the centerback, fullback, attacking midfielder, and winger on the same side, and the zone between the centerbacks and attacking midfielders. As we have analyzed, the spaces out wide are usually occupied by the wingers or by a member of the second line who can step up. In the case of the zones between the lines, the members of the back line are responsible for constricting this space and preventing the opponents from turning.

Generally, the two centerbacks cover these three spaces. Against opponents with only one attacker, the marking defender follows the opposing forward if he drops down to support, as seen in Image 152. Meanwhile the other centerback, here Matip (32) on the right, steps up on the opponent between the lines to try and intercept the ball. Against opponents who play with two center forwards fixing the centerbacks, these defenders simply mark their players.

In situations like the one in Image 152, if a pass is threaded into space on one side and the centerback on that side is fixed by an opponent, it's the fullback in that channel who moves out to the opponent within his zone. This demonstrates the aggressiveness of Klopp's players when the ball enters their defensive structure. It's a team that has no qualms about defending from the front.

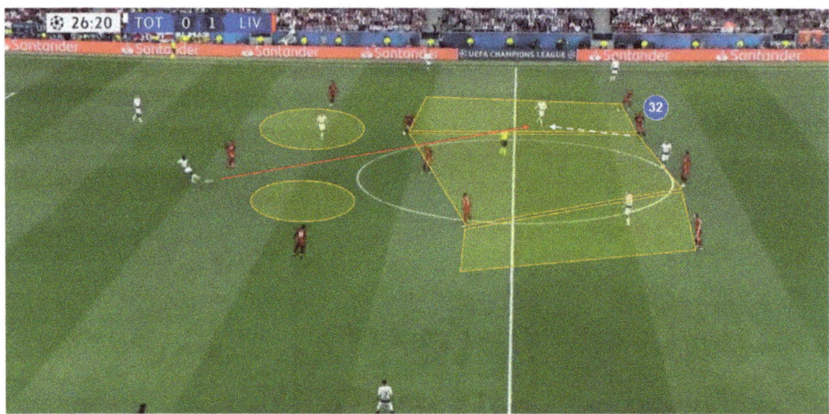

Image 152. Champions League final 2018/19: Tottenham–Liverpool

To keep the middle block tight, the defenders are required to stay high up the field. This results in increased space in the zone of offensive advantage, something that opponents can exploit. When faced with the threat of (or an actual situation of) direct play into space, the entire line must have their bodies profiled correctly in relation to the area where the ball will land and be prepared to run backwards. As seen in Image 153, if the ball goes to an outer channel, the entire line will be oriented towards that channel. On the other hand, if the ball goes to an inside channel the fullback on that side faces the closest centerback and the rest of the defense will be oriented towards the ball.

153. Champions League final 2018/19: Tottenham–Liverpool

When competing for a ball after a long delivery from the opponent, Klopp's Liverpool forms a 3 + 1 structure. Image 154 outlines this concept, with a centerback stepping up for the aerial duel, in this case Van Dijk (4) on the left, and the other three members of the back line: the right centerback Matip (32) and the fullbacks, Robertson (26) on the left and Alexander-Arnold (66) on the right, dropping back from their positions to cover.

In the event that the initial duel is lost and a second duel takes place, the other centerback, who is Matip (32) in this action, will be the next player to challenge. For their part, the two fullbacks remain tucked in behind in a 2 + 1 structure. This process is continually repeated until they can take possession of the ball.

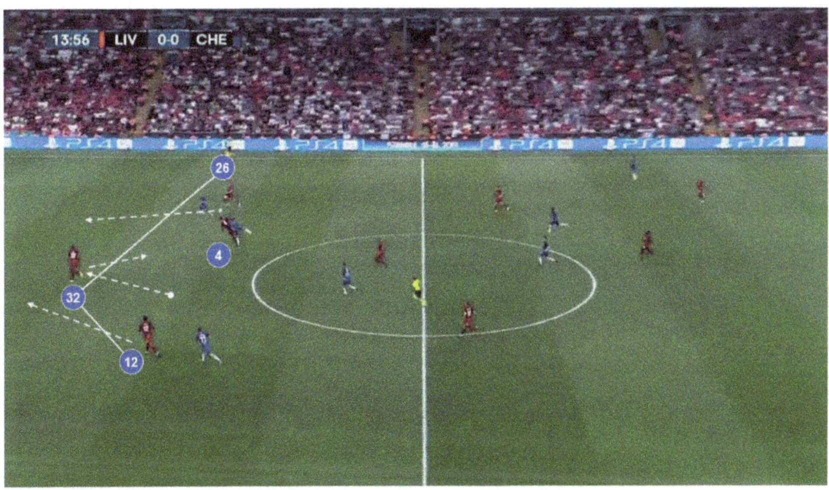

Image 154. European Super Cup 2019/20: Liverpool–Chelsea

LOW BLOCK

To defend in a low block, Klopp's Liverpool maintains the same system as in a medium block; a zonal 1-4-5-1. The difference is that in this part of the field the wingers permanently drop down to join the midfield line. In these situations, only the center forward is exempt from defensive functions behind the ball. This player is responsible for being the long outlet for the ball when it leaves the recovery zone after gaining possession.

As can be seen in Image 155, the shifting towards the ball to prevent progression follows the same principles as in a medium block: the player in the channel where the ball is, here the right attacking midfielder Oxlade-Chamberlain (21), drops off the player in possession and returns to his position in the line once the ball moves to a different channel. At that moment it's the defensive midfielder, in this case Henderson (14), who steps up to the ball in the new channel. These movements toward the ball are intended to put the player on the ball under pressure, slow down the opponent's progression, and keep the ball as far away from the goal as possible. Often this will force the ball to be passed backwards.

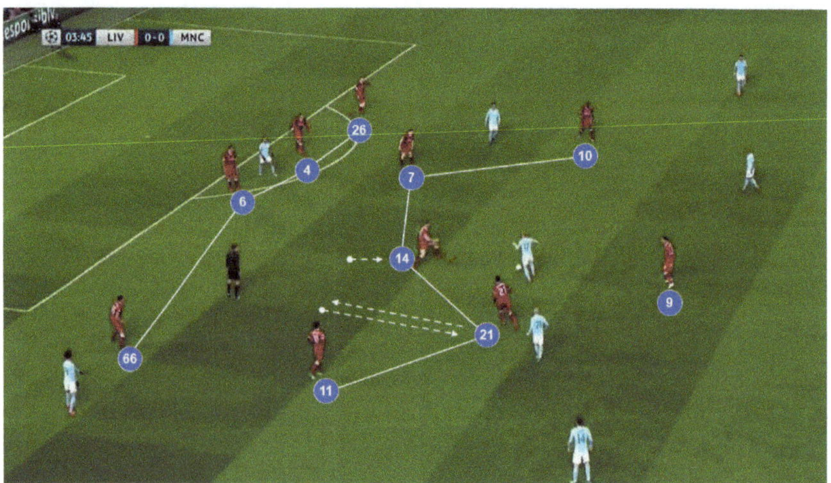

Image 155. Champions League quarter-final 2017/18:
Liverpool–Manchester City

The sequence of behaviors for Klopp's Liverpool in each situation is as follows: when the opponent passes horizontally, the player in the same channel as the ball will step up; when the opponent plays backwards, the block advances; when the opponent makes a forward pass inside, the block drops back and closes in on the central channel; and when the opponent looks to connect out wide, a nearby player behind the ball must step up to the opponent with the ball in the outside channel.

As can be seen in Image 156, most of the time it's the fullback on the active side, Alexander-Arnold (66) on this occasion, who steps up. A 3 + 1 structure is maintained in the back line, since the other members (the two central defenders and the fullback on the weak side) stay to protect the center and maintain an adequate distance between themselves. The fullback's movement to the outside means that the interval between him and the centerback increases significantly, presenting a very attractive space for the opponents to attack. Therefore the attacking midfielder on the strong side, here Oxlade-Chamberlain (21), is responsible for covering or following the opponent who attacks that gap. In this way, the opponent only eliminates one player if the fullback is overcome by the ball.

If the centerback on the strong side has to cover the teammate who steps up, the space that would open the widest would be the interval between the centerbacks. In this situation there is a risk that two players, instead of one, could be overtaken by the ball.

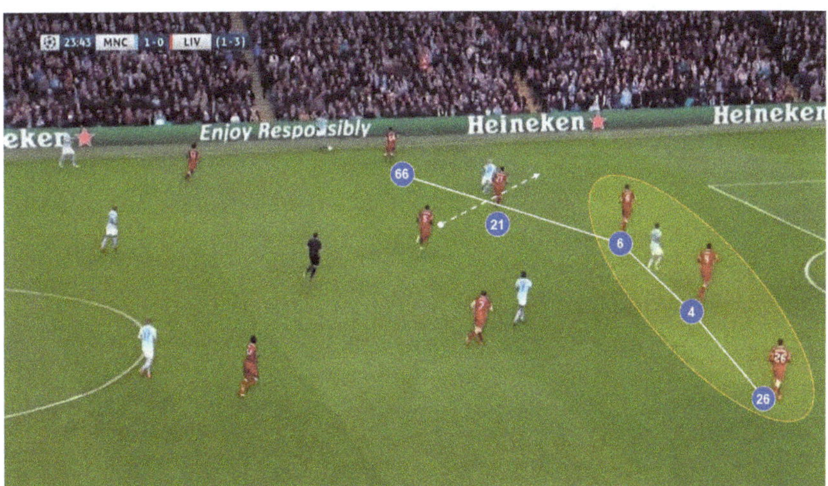

Image 156. Champions League quarter-final 2017/18:
Manchester City–Liverpool

The only situation in which the centerbacks go out wide is when the opposing center forward attacks the interval between a centerback and a fullback and there is no possibility for a midfielder, be it an attacking or defensive midfielder, to pursue him. Image 157 demonstrates this in an action in which Lovren (6), the centerback on the active side, follows the opposing center forward as he dismarks into the interval between himself and the right fullback Alexander-Arnold (66).

Once the fullback has been overtaken by the ball, the compensatory movement proposed by Klopp in these situations is for him to exchange positions with the centerback. As an alternative, one of the midfielders can also take his place.

Image 157. Champions League final 2017/18: Real Madrid–
Liverpool

However, in numbers-down situations where the opponent has an extra player, the fullback doesn't step up. As can be seen in the 2-vs-3 action in Image 158, the fullback on the active side, in this case the right back Alexander-Arnold (66), does not move towards the penultimate attacker, here the left back David Alaba (27), because that would leave space behind him that could be attacked by the left winger Franck Ribéry (7) or the attacking midfielder James Rodríguez (11). Instead Alexander-Arnold (66), the fullback in that zone, looks to delay until help can arrive in the form of the winger or the attacking midfielder from that side.

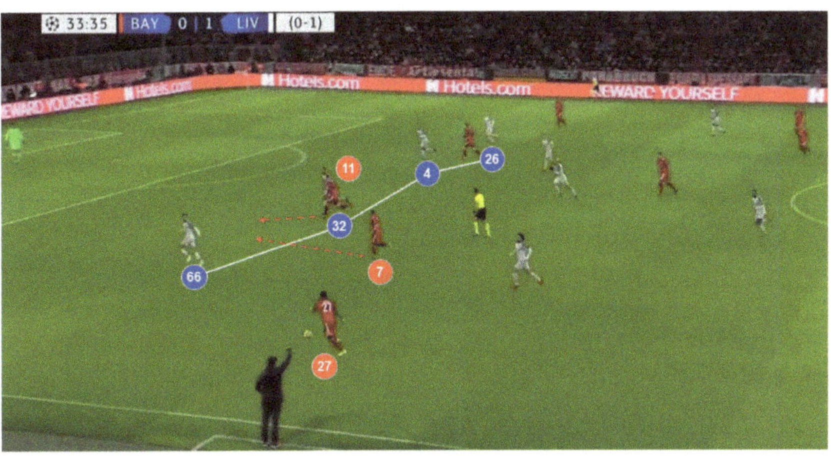

Image 158. Champions League quarter-final 2018/19: Bayern München–Liverpool

We have previously seen that the fullback often moves into the outside channel, since the winger has to travel a greater distance to retreat to his fallback position and is often overtaken by the ball. However, as can be seen in Image 159, the ideal defensive situation for Klopp is to have his winger, in this case Mané (10) on the left, step up to pressure instead of the fullback, here Robertson (26). This is because it's better to mobilize a player from the second line rather than one from the last line.

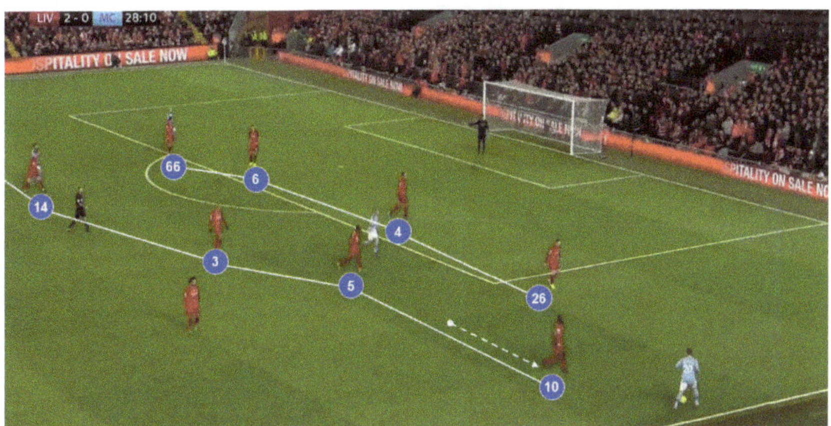

Image 159. Premier League 2019/20: Liverpool–Manchester City

Another defensive key for Klopp's Liverpool is the consistency that the two central defenders have when defending the penalty area. When one of them gets out of position, it becomes a moment of vulnerability. For this reason, the German coach is a great strategist when it comes to implementing systems for support and coverage in all contexts. He applies the same mechanisms with the Reds that were previously applied during his time at Borussia Dortmund, but with the advantage of having an additional midfielder.

As Image 160 shows, this allows the team to create numerical superiorities or equalities on the outside. In the case of a 4-vs-3 situation the left winger on the active side, a role temporarily played by the center forward Firmino (9) in this sequence, and the defensive midfielder Wijnaldum (5) will support the left back Robertson (26). Meanwhile, the left attacking midfielder Milner (7) will cover inside. In this way, Liverpool keeps their two centerbacks Van Dijk (4) and Lovren (6) inside the penalty area without altering their 3 + 2 structure.

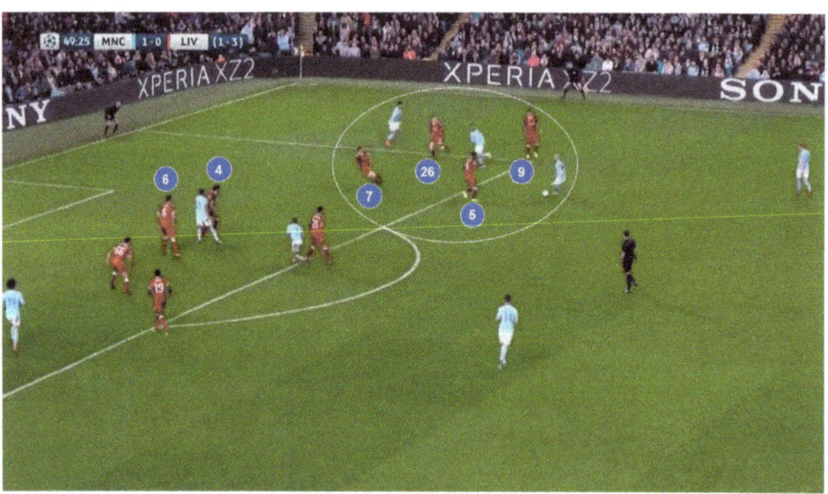

Image 160. Champions League quarter-final 2017/18:
Manchester City–Liverpool

At Liverpool, Klopp also uses the same defensive scheme in the penalty area that he employed at Borussia Dortmund. As can be seen in Image 161, the fullback on the active side, who in this action is Alexander-Arnold (66), steps up to the player with the ball to plug up the middle and cover Henderson (14), the attacking midfielder on that side. Inside the penalty area the team defends in a 3 + 2 zonal structure: the closest centerback, Matip (32) on the right, occupies the area at the near post; the other centerback, Van Dijk (4) on the left, covers the area near the penalty spot, and the weak side fullback, Robertson (26) on the left, covers the far post. The other two midfielders, the defensive midfielder Fabinho (3), and the left attacking midfielder Milner (7), protect the top of the penalty area.

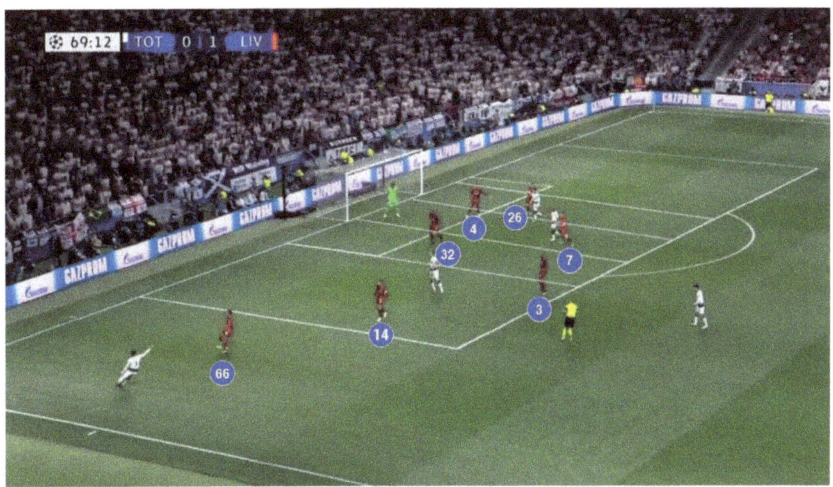

Image 161. Champions League final 2018/19: Tottenham–Liverpool

Defensive transition

As explained above, the *gegenpressing* practiced by Klopp's Borussia Dortmund could be considered as the incubation process of this concept. However, it's as a result of his work at Liverpool that *gegenpressing* was consolidated into a truly effective tactic. The German coach has made these refinements by exerting greater influence in the final third of the field and through a more rational offensive positioning that takes the defensive transition into consideration.

In certain statistical parameters, it can be seen how Klopp's Liverpool is better optimized in the offensive phase than Borussia Dortmund was. In his first six seasons with the English team he achieved an average possession rate of 58.1%, with a passing efficiency rate of 83.4%. In comparison, with the German team he averaged 52.3% and 77.2%, respectively. In addition, during that same period at Liverpool 31.5% of the total passes were made in the final third of the field, while at Borussia Dortmund that number was 29.5%.

These statistics from the offensive phase help us to understand the greatest impact of *gegenpressing* at Klopp's Liverpool. Accumulating a greater number of passes in the final third before losing the ball means that players are in their planned locations and better prepared when they lose the ball, with more favorable distances between them. All of this contributes to the opponent having less space when they win the ball back.

Teams that carry out *gegenpressing* organize themselves not only to score goals, but also to be properly positioned to press at the moment they lose the ball. As can be seen in Image 162, the positioning of Klopp's Borussia Dortmund meant having a 4 + 2 structure in the inside channels, with four forwards in the first line of pressure and two midfielders who would be staggered at different heights on the vertical axis. During the defensive transition, the two central midfielders were normally the players who remained behind the ball while the ones who pressed the ball stayed up higher. This left them in a demanding situation: at least one of the two had to step up to press the player in possession, which meant taking the risk that the opponents would exploit the free space to their sides after winning the ball.

The behaviors of the fullbacks were another influential factor in the lack of effectiveness of the *gegenpressing* at Klopp's Borussia Dortmund. When the ball was lost and these players were high and ahead of the ball, the threat of the opposing counterattack made them more likely to drop back rather than to immediately press the player in possession. When they were behind the ball, they could defend up high more often when the ball was lost.

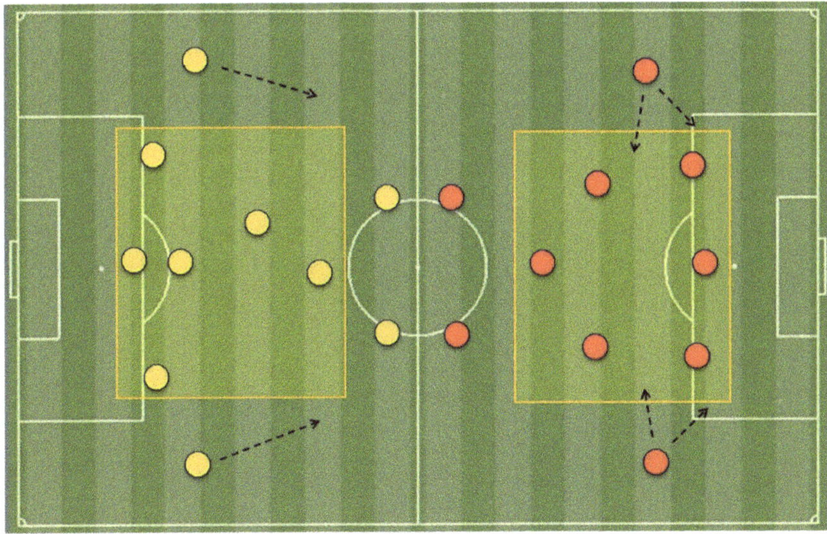

Image 162. Differences in positioning during the finishing phase between Klopp's Borussia Dortmund (left) and Liverpool (right). Author's work

But Klopp has made minor modifications at Liverpool to make *gegenpressing* a less impulsive and more streamlined tactic. The change of formation to include three strikers has given him a more balanced positional structure. As can be seen in Image 162, Klopp's Liverpool has a 3 + 3 structure in the interior channels. This equalizes the two lines numerically and favors the establishment of defensive triangles. The width of the field is dealt with more rationally and the team is better protected to provide support and coverage. When losing the ball in the central channel, the players are prepared to press the player with the ball inside.

To improve the activation of Klopp's players at Liverpool, he also had to change the mentality of the fullbacks while they were high up the field. Even if they are ahead of the ball, their first option is usually to press up front or to the inside after losing possession.

This is one of the great attractions that *gegenpressing* offers the player: the ability to attack without the ball.

The action in Image 163 serves as an example: three of the players who are ahead of the ball when it's lost, the attacking midfielder Firmino (9), the right winger Shaqiri (23), and the left back Robertson (26), press to the inside. By activating quickly, they are able to pressure the player with the ball from multiple directions.

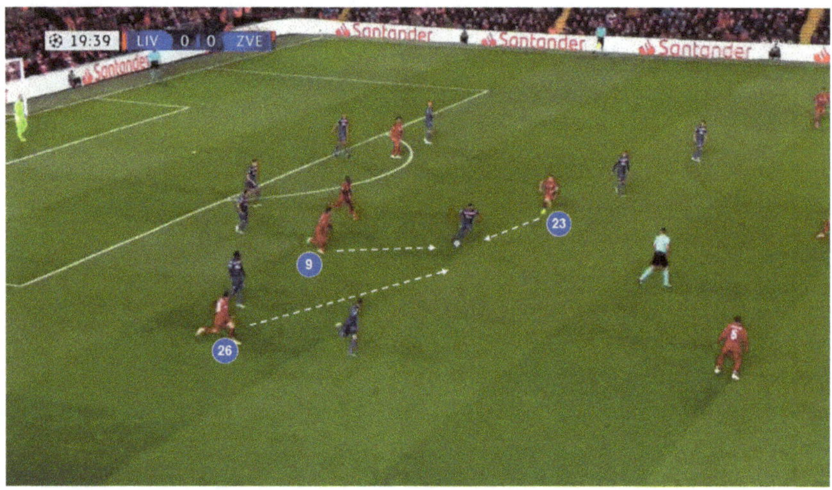

Image 163. Champions League group stage 2018/19: Liverpool–
Red Star

As can be seen in Image 164, the 1-2-3-5 arrangement in the finishing phase allows for the formation of inverted triangles in 2 + 1 microstructures, just like at Klopp's Borussia Dortmund. In this action the left attacking midfielder Wijnaldum (5), temporarily playing on the right, and the right winger Salah (11) press the player in possession together with the help of the player overtaken by the ball, the right back Alexander-Arnold (66), to force the opponent to play the ball backwards. Meanwhile, the right attacking midfielder Can (23) is protecting the area at the bottom apex of the triangle.

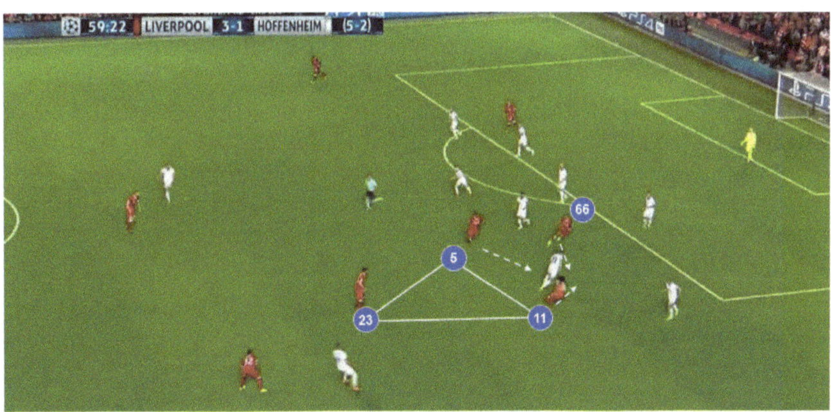

Image 164. Champions League qualifying round 2017/18:
Liverpool–Hoffenheim

Klopp's Liverpool also carries out *gegenpressing* with 1 + 2 triangular microstructures. Image 165 reflects an action in which an advanced player, the right attacking midfielder Henderson (14), initiates the pressure due to his proximity when the ball is lost. In this type of maneuver the other two players nearby, the center forward Origi (27) and the right back Alexander-Arnold (66) in this example, will resolve the situation based on the position of the ball and according to how they anticipate the next pass.

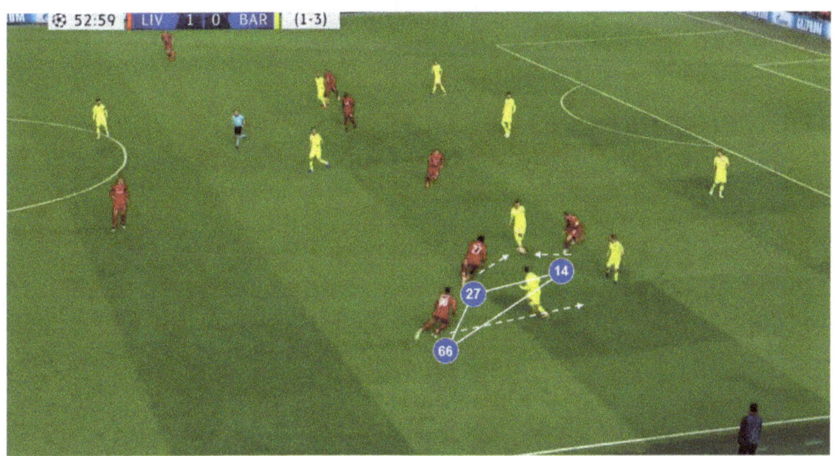

Image 165. Champions League semi-final 2018/19: Liverpool–
Barcelona

Klopp's Liverpool also executes gegenpressing when playing direct. When under pressure or unable to progress by playing short, the Reds can play long towards the opponent's back line and press the ball when it drops. In these situations the opponent will have their lines deep in the opponent's half of the field, so the area of offensive advantage is greater. As can be seen in Image 166, two players, here the right winger Mané (19) and the center forward Firmino (9), put pressure on the ball as it drops. If they are able to regain possession, the field is open for them to reach the opponent's goal in very favorable conditions.

Image 166. Premier League 2016/17: Liverpool–Tottenham

A fundamental aspect for successful *gegenpressing* is the ability of the players who stay back to anticipate the play. As Lijnders (2022) explains: "Without joint pressure, without smothering the opponent, pressing after losing the ball makes no sense". In Klopp's teams, both the central defenders and the center midfielders are very aggressive, marking opponents who drop back to support the ball. Eliminating that potential option to play long allows them to remain in the opponent's half of the field longer without the need to fall back. However, if pressing after losing the ball is not successful, the entire team will retreat.

At Liverpool, just like during his time at Borussia Dortmund, Klopp's team has two methods of dropping back with three players, both prioritizing the central channel. As can be seen in Image 167, one option is for the fullback on the weak side to drop back, in this case Alexander-Arnold (66) on the right, along with the two centerbacks. If both fullbacks had moved up during the previous attack, it's the defensive midfielder, in this example Henderson (14), who maintains the three-player superiority, as shown in Image 168.

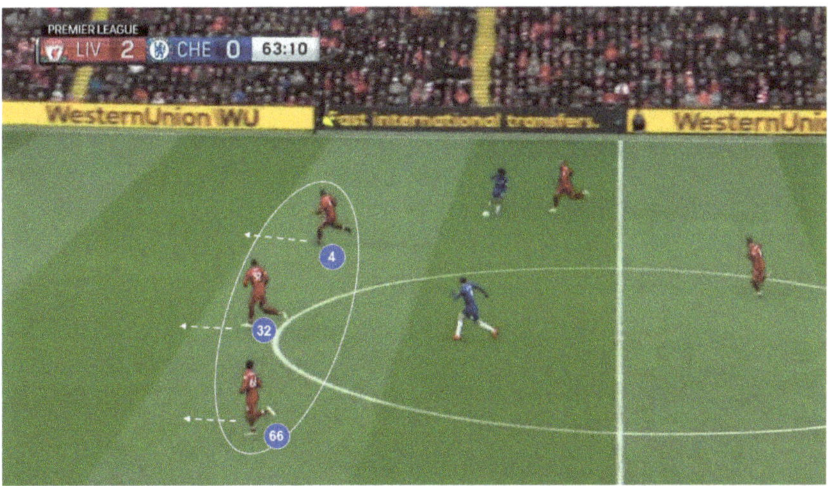

Image 167. Premier League 2018/19: Liverpool–Chelsea

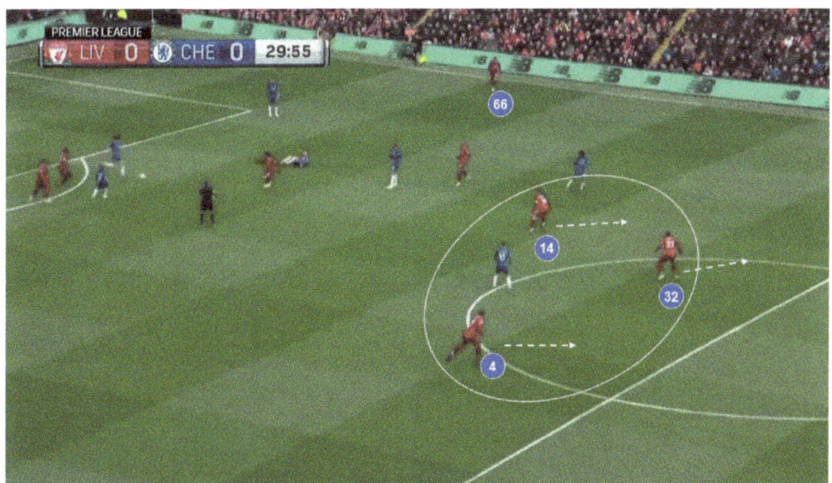

Image 168. Premier League 2018/19: Liverpool–Chelsea

Training activities inspired by Klopp's game model

POSITIONAL GAME FOR BUILDING OUT OF THE BACK

Objectives	Movements for building out of the back; third man; breaking lines; free man, and speed of play.				
N.º of players	13	Space	35x55 m.	Duration	2 series of 10'
Equipment	4 tall cones, 4 flat cones and 2 mini-goals.				

The activity

Two teams face each other in an 8-vs-5 situation in a playing area divided into two zones. In the first zone, the team in possession plays with a 3-vs-1 superiority. In the second zone the teams play 5-vs-5. The attacking team (red) score in the mini-goals (simulating an inside pass) or by dribbling between the cones (simulating a fullback running with the ball). Play restarts from the goalkeeper. The white team finishes on goal if they win the ball.

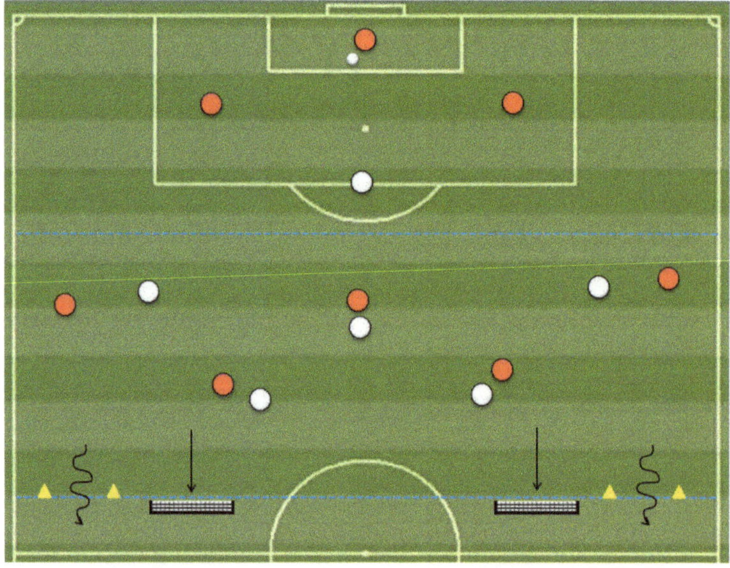

Variations

Adapt the structure of the defending team to the opponent's system and allow one or more additional defenders to enter the first zone.

Coaching points

Insist on the movements you want to see in the starting zone.

Identify the free man.

Support the ball with the proper body orientation.

THREE-TEAM RONDO

Objectives	Third man; play the way you face; free man; speed of play; rapid progression; support, and wall passes.

N.º of players	15	Space	30x20 m.	Duration	3 series of 5'

Equipment	8 cones.

The activity

Organize three teams of five players (5-vs-5 plus 5) in a space marked out with two zones and a central strip. The three groups are arranged as follows: one in possession (red) in the first zone; one out of possession (white) with three players in the first zone and two in the central strip, and the third team (yellow) with two players in the central strip and three waiting in the far zone. Score by connecting three passes in the first zone and then triangulating via a third man action with a player in the central strip or the opposite zone. When that happens, repeat the procedure in the second zone. The two yellow players from the central strip join their teammates and two members from the other team in possession (red) take their place. Play with a two-touch limit. The defending team (white) must recover the ball and earns a point if, after gaining possession, they triangulate with a third man action. The team that loses the ball must press in their zone.

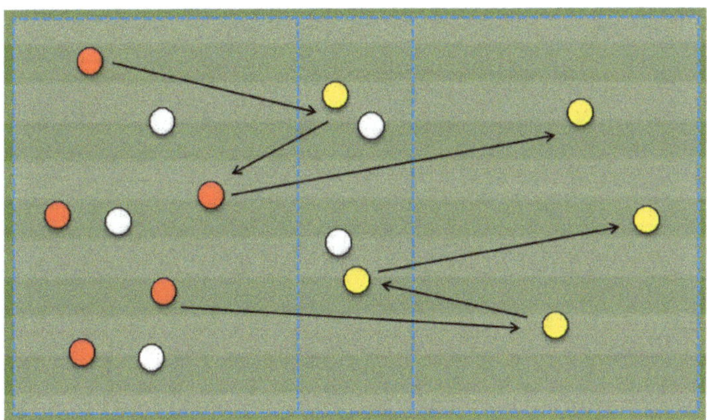

Coaching points

Progress by performing a third man action.
Play vertical passes to the more distant players: you must to look for the far players to find the near players.
Play the way you face: don't turn when you do not know if you're free.
Staggering the positioning of the players to avoid having several players in the same channel or at the same height.

POSITIONAL GAME WITH FINISHING

Objectives	Third man; playing to the far players (skipping lines); free man; wall passes; speed of play; dismarking; finishing, and support.				
N.º of players	20	Space	Half a field	Duration	20'
Equipment	14 cones and 1 goal.				

The activity

Two teams play 7-vs-6 in a 30x40 m playing area. In front of the penalty area is a strip with three zones for the three forwards. These players may not enter the first zone. In order to finish, the team in possession (red) must play to one of the forwards. These forwards can turn and finish, look for a through-pass inside, or play a third-man action into the corner for the fullback to cross the ball into a 3-vs-3 situation in the box. There are always three defenders to protect the penalty area. Only one defender can step up into the forwards' zone to prevent a turn or intercept the ball. The defending team scores in the mini-goal if they win the ball.

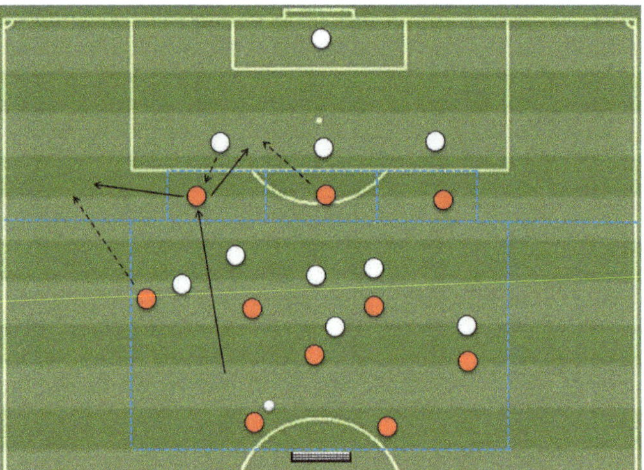

Variations

Work on different movements to break into the finishing zone.
Allow one or more additional attackers to advance into the finsihing zone.

Coaching points

Thread passes to the farther players (the forwards).
Look to play into the corners of the field.
Forwards should link their dismarking movements into the finishing zone.
Players should make their movements in the penalty area in anticipation of the cross from the fullback.

CONDITIONED GAME	
Objectives	Third man; wall passes; switching play; speed of play; dismarking; finishing, and support.

N.º of players	22	Space	Half a field	Duration	20'
Equipment	8 cones and 1 goal.				

The activity

Two teams play 11-vs-11 in half a field. The playing area is divided into three channels, with the outer channels divided further into two offensive corners. Only two attackers and one defender can enter these zones, to generate superiorities of 2-vs-1 or 3-vs-2 in triangles in the outer channels. A goal scored after triangulation in a corner is worth double; a goal after a switch of play from one corner to the other counts triple.

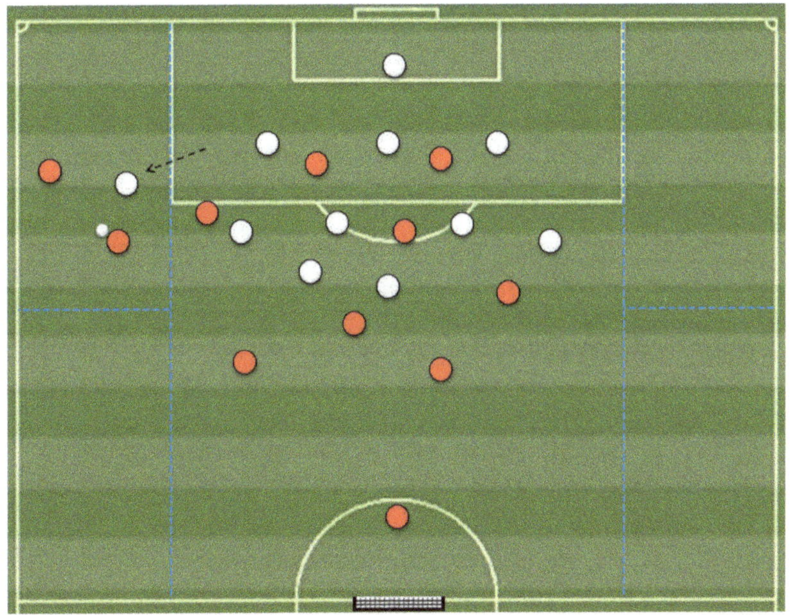

Coaching points

Attackers should create 2-vs-1 and 3-vs-2 situations.
Players should make their movements in the penalty area in anticipation of the cross from the fullback.

SUPERIORITY WAVE GAME

Objectives	Counterattack; wall passes; dismarking; fixing opponents, and finishing.				
N.º of players	Unlimited	Space	32x40 m.	Duration	20'
Equipment	4 cones and 2 goals.				

The activity

In a double penalty area, two teams face each other in waves of 2-vs-1 superiority. The player from the attacking team who does not shoot stays on to defend. The sequence for the players is attack-defend-rest.

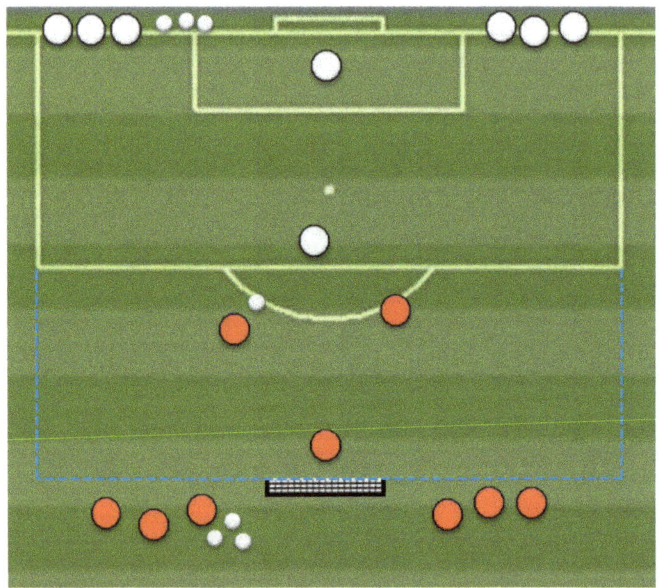

Variations

Outline and explain the movements desired in the offensive transition.
Play 3-vs-2 or 4-vs-3. If using three attackers, divide the playing area into three channels which must each be occupied until reaching the opposing penalty area.
Add neutral players on the sides.

Coaching points

Insist the players carry out specific movements in the offensive transition.
Fix an opponent before passing.
Adjust the timing of the pass and the position of the receiver to avoid straying offside.
Finish quickly.

PROGRESSION AND FINISHING GAME

Objectives	Counterattack; exiting the recovery zone; wall passes; dismarking; fixing opponents, and finishing.

N.º of players	14	Space	Half a field	Duration	20'
Equipment	4 cones and 1 goal.				

The activity

The activity starts in a 15x15 m playing area with two teams facing each other in a 4-vs-4 plus 2 possession game. The two exterior neutrals have two roles: to provide outside support during possession and, after winning the ball, to be attackers and finishers (acting as wingers). Out of possession, there are three defenders and a center forward on standby. After recovering the ball, there are two ways to exit the ball recovery zone. The first is to combine with a neutral on the outside, who dribbles forward into the middle and generates a 3-vs-3 counterattack as quickly as possible (with the forward and the other neutral). The other way is to play to the supporting center forward who lays the ball off to one of the two neutrals to create the 3-vs-3 counterattack as quickly as possible.

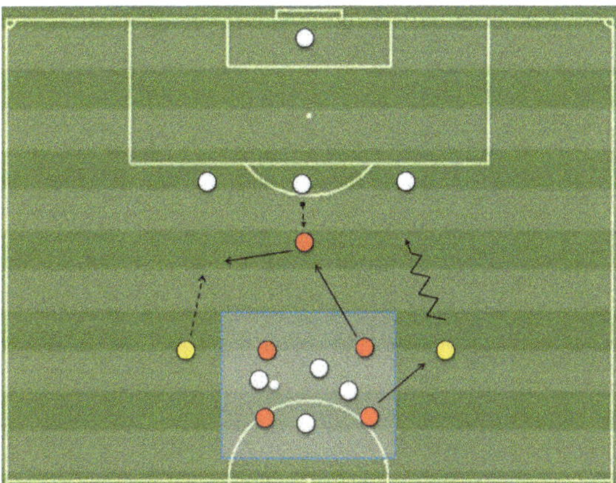

Variations

One of the defenders drops back to defend the counterattack in a 4-vs-3.
Only one of the neutrals joins the counterattack (2-vs-3).
One attacker joins the counterattack to create a 4-vs-3.
One attacker and one defender can join the counterattack, creating a 4-vs-4.

Coaching points

Emphasize the importance of the exit pass from the recovery zone.
Attack through the three channels.
Insist on specific movements in the offensive transition.

POSITIONAL GAME				
Objectives	Closing passing lines; narrowing defensive intervals; penetrating the zones; shifting; covering; interceptions, and overcoming pressure.			
N.º of players	12	**Space** 20x12 m.	**Duration**	3 series of 5'
Equipment	15 cones and 4 mini-goals.			

The activity

Two teams play 6-vs-6 in an area divided into eight squares. The groups are arranged in 4 + 2 structures. In the line of four, each player operates in one square (representing the channels). The line of two has the freedom of movement horizontally to move between zones, but only behind the opponent's line of four. The objective of the team in possession is to score a goal by threading a pass to either of the two teammates behind the opponent's defense. These two players must play 1-touch and both must touch the ball before scoring (via a third man movement). The team out of possession must prevent the opponent from breaking the lines. The defender who is in the same channel as the ball must press the player in possession. The other three defenders must narrow the intervals to cover the passing lines and avoid being overcome. If the defenders are overcome by the ball, they must drop back to prevent a goal. None of the players in the back line can invade the opponent's half of the field. Possession changes when the opponent recovers the ball.

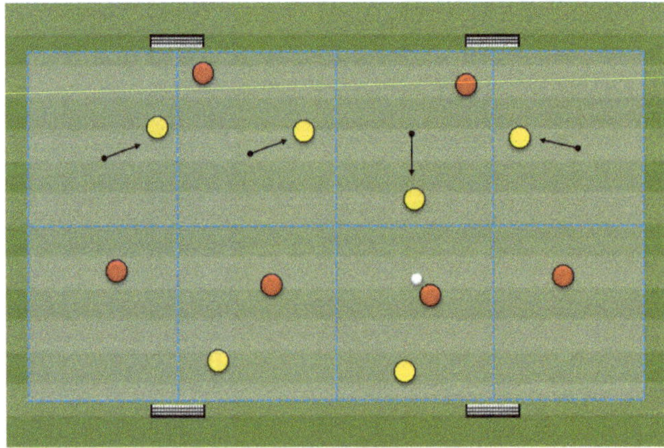

Coaching points

Step up to press and block the vertical passing lines.
Narrow the defensive intervals.
Adjust the defensive line to cover when a player steps up.
Press if a player is overtaken by the ball.
A correct body profile is important.

ATTACKING-DEFENDING

Objectives	Closing passing lines; narrowing defensive intervals; penetrating the zones; shifting; covering; and defending the penalty area.				
N.º of players	12	Space	40x30 m.	Duration	2 series of 10'
Equipment	4 cones.				

The activity

Two teams face each other in a 6-vs-5 plus Goalkeeper situation. The defensive subsystem is arranged as a 4-1; the offensive subsystem as a 3-3. The attacking team advances on goal while the other defends according to the principles explained in the low block section of this book.

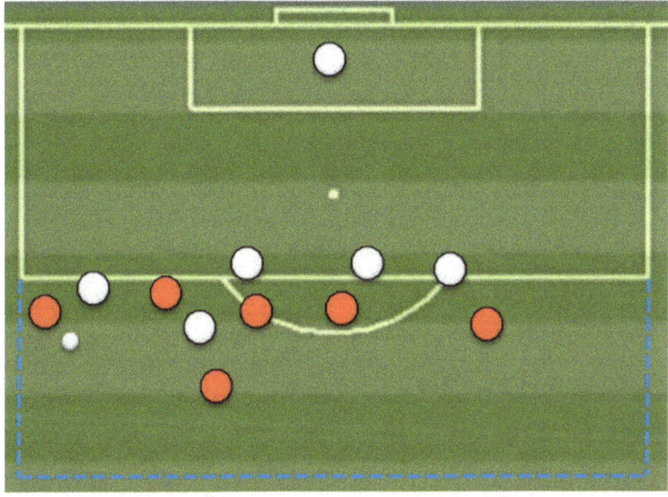

Variations

Include an offensive neutral.
Increase the number of players to create a 10-vs-9 in half a field.
Set up two mini-goals for the defenders to score on after winning the ball.

Coaching points

Maintain the 3 + 1 structure when the fullback steps up.
Guard against the supporting actions of the defensive midfielder.
The block needs to move according to the position of the ball.
The height of the line is set by the ball-side centerback.
A correct body profile is important.

TRANSITIONAL RONDO

Objectives	Pressure after losing the ball; closing passing lines; covering, and exchanging positions.				
N.º of players	12	Space	15x15 m.	Duration	3 series of 8'
Equipment	8 cones and 4 mini-goals.				

The activity

Organize three teams of four players. In the first 8x8 m grid, a 4-vs-2 takes place. The offensive team (red) must keep the ball, while the defensive team (yellow) must recover it. When the defensive team wins the ball, the team that loses possession must enter the grid to press and tries to score in one of the four outside mini-goals if they win it back. At the moment the red team recovers, the waiting team (white) must enter to press, together with the two inside players (yellow). After several repetitions, change the inside players. The three teams rotate roles after every series.

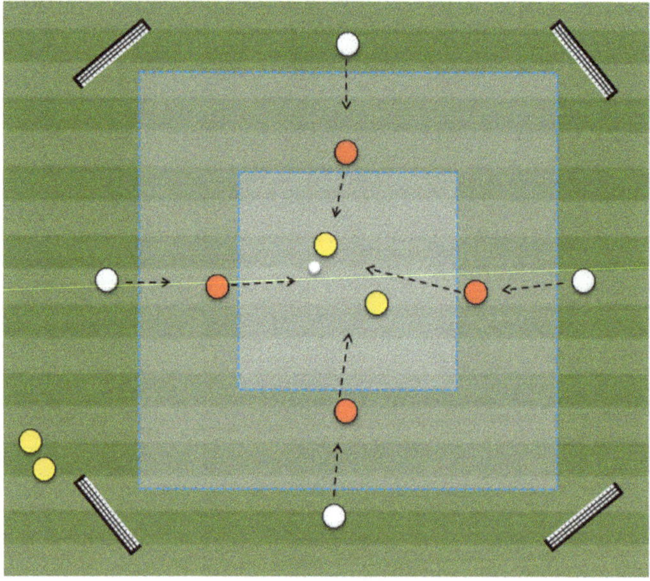

Variations

Include another player in the first phase (4-vs-3) to work on positional exchanges in the 2 + 1 and 1-2 triangular micro-structures.

Coaching points

Activation after losing the ball. Switches of play.
Press the ball in triangular 2 + 1 and 1 + 2 micro-structures.

CONDITIONED GAME

Objectives	Pressure after losing the ball; closing passing lines; narrowing defensive intervals; penetrating the zones; shifting; covering, and defending the penalty area.				
N.º of players	22	Space	Half a field	Duration	20'
Equipment	6 cones.				

The activity

Two teams face each other in a playing area divided into three zones. A goal scored after recovering the ball in the pressing zone is worth triple.

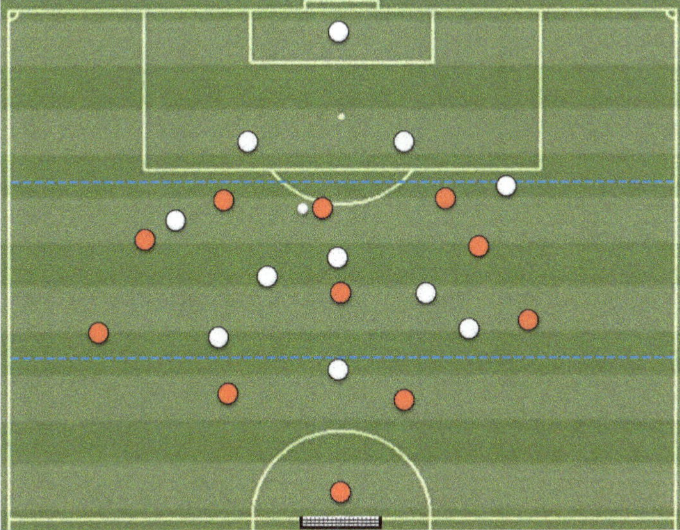

Variations

Teams have 6 seconds to score after winning the ball.

Coaching points

Press the player in possession in triangular 2 + 1 and 1 + 2 micro-structures.
The forwards should move and dismark into space after their team wins the ball.

ABOUT THE AUTHOR

Alejandro Gómez Escolar (born September 10, 1997 in Madrid) is a sports journalist and football coach for the Royal Football Federation of Madrid, specializing in tactical analysis and scouting. He has been a member of the coaching staffs, as a coach and analyst, of several teams at the highest levels of grassroots football in the Madrid area.

Bibliography

Aracil, Sergio (May 7th, 2020). *Juego de posición con finalización.* [Video file]. YouTube. https://youtu.be/BwzBzXriTA8

Aracil, Sergio (February 14th, 2022). *Ejercicio para mejorar la salida de balón en fútbol 11 (y fútbol 7).* [Video file]. YouTube. https://youtu.be/0CgPUSC9GBs

Bretones, Andrés (August 3rd, 2021). Movimientos tácticos y espacios en salida de balón con el sistema 1-4-3-3. *Andrés Bretones.* https://andresbretones.com/movimientos-tacticos-y-espacios-en-salida-de-balon-con-el-sistema-1-4-3-3/

Cano, Óscar (2012). *El juego de posición del FC Barcelona.* Vigo. MCSports.

Cervera, Adrián (2020). *El juego de Aproximación. Independently published.*

Cox, Michael (2019). *Zonal Marking. The Making of Modern European Football.* London. HarperCollins.

Egurza, Mikel (October 9th, 2020). *Comportamientos de una línea defensiva formada por 4 defensores.* [Video file]. YouTube. https://youtu.be/O7VuhmSlTy8

Emery, Unai [VideosEmery] (August 18th, 2010). *Conferencia de Unai Emery (1/5).* [Video file]. YouTube. https://youtu.be/BfuU5Nkfy3o

Footbalia (no date). *Footbalia.* https://footballia.net/

Fullmatchsport (no date). *Fullmatchsport.* https://fullmatchsports.cc/

Guardiola, Pep [Fut Bol] (October 9th, 2016). *Pep Guardiola sobre la presión: "siempre hay que estar entre dos posiciones".* [Video file]. YouTube. https://youtu.be/hgIMTwdfMNw

Honigstein, Raphael (no date). La pasión de Klopp. *Goal.* https://www.goal.com/story/la-pasion-de-klopp/

Klopp, Jürgen [*Sky Sports Retro*] (September 28th, 2020). *Jürgen Klopp explains the importance of gegenpressing.* [Video file]. YouTube. https://youtu.be/XvHT3BJu7g4

Klopp, Jürgen [*Taktikr*] (March 14th, 2017). *Jürgen Klopp zum Thema Gegenpressing.* [Video file]. YouTube. https://youtu.be/m9QeDltVlMY

Klopp, Jürgen [*Western Union*] (May 29th, 2019). *Jürgen Klopp - The Interview | Klopp reveals how to succeed.* [Video file]. YouTube. https://youtu.be/mR2N3o9noFM

Lijnders, Pepijn [*The Coaches' Voice*] (April 28th, 2022). *Pep Lijnders • Champions League Tactics, @Liverpool FC 4 Barcelona 0 • Masterclass.* [Video file]. YouTube. https://youtu.be/zlwVZTtR0zQ

Marić, René (October 7th, 2014). *Gegen- oder Gegenpressing. Spielverlagerung.de.* https://spielverlagerung.com/2014/10/07/counter-or-gegenpressing/

Marić, René (August 22nd, 2015). *Taktiktheorie: Das Gegenpressing. Spielverlagerung.de.* https://spielverlagerung.de/2015/07/22/taktiktheorie-das-gegenpressing/

Mere [Diario As] (February 5th, 2020) *Mere explica y desarrolla las transiciones en el fútbol actual.* [Video file]. YouTube. https://youtu.be/QUGOVAAzAFc

Moreno, Robert (2013). *Mi "receta" del 4-4-2.* FutbolDLibro.

Neveling, Elmar (2016). *Jürgen Klopp. The Biography.* London. *Ebury Press.*

Osmanbašić, Adin (June 1st, 2015). *Pressing, Counterpressing and counterattacking. The Tactical Room.* https://www.martiperarnau.com/pressing-counterpressing-and-counterattacking/

Soriano, Enric (Octuber 9th, 2020). *Cursos MIR4R – Plan de partido ante presión alta Liverpool. Fragmento ocupación base.* [Archivo de video]. YouTube. https://youtu.be/l0P2nCzRlE0

Soriano, Enric (February 24th, 2021). *PONENCIA – Interacciones que nacen de las estructuras de juego. Ejemplo con sistema 1-3-4-1-2*. [Video file]. YouTube. https://youtu.be/ruY2TZ6iBZA

Transfermarkt (no date). *Transfermarkt*. https://www.transfermarkt.es/

Vissers, Willem (January 2nd, 2017). Pepijn Lijnders: "Hierna wil ik hoofdtrainer zijn, liefst in Nederland". *De Volkskrant*. https://www.volkskrant.nl/sport/hierna-wil-ik-hoofdtrainer-zijn-liefst-in-nederland~b2d8379a/

Whoscored (no date). *Whoscored*. https://es.whoscored.com/

YouCoach (2019). *Liverpool Tactical Analysis*. Monselice. YouCoach.